Ms. Ageless America

By Marilyn Gail Gaw

Cover design by Aaron Smith
Illustrations by Kevin Nordstrom
Editing & Design by Grammar Goddess Editing

ISBN Hardcover: 978-0-9994644-0-3
ISBN Paperback: 978-0-9994644-2-7
ISBN Ebook: 978-0-9994644-1-0

This book is dedicated to my editor, Sarah, without whose encouragement this book would never have been born; to Richard, my soulmate (most of the time) for always being there and for just "getting" me; to my lovely mother, who was the first "ageless woman" I ever knew; and to all the ageless women I know and all the ageless women I've yet to meet.

Table of Contents

INTRODUCTION

THIS BOOK WAS WRITTEN for "real women" of every age, from 19 to 99. It is a book all about you. YOU are Ms. Ageless America. It is not meant for beauty queens, rich, pampered, or idle women, ladies who only "do lunch," vain women who are obsessed with their age, or bored socialites. It is not about women who have nothing but time and money to chase endless youth, although these women are certainly welcome to read the book if they would like to learn a thing or two about "real beauty."

No, this book is about you, your mother, your grandmother, your sister, your best friend. This book is about real women, real life, and real actions that can be done every day to address aging. This book can show you the way to becoming an ageless woman at any age.

Like many things in life, such as fine wine, classic cars, and first edition books, "ageless women" get more valuable with time. But unlike these items, real beauty is not something that can be purchased or acquired. It is something each and every one of us already has within us. We all want to be and look young and healthy, but as each decade passes, it gets more challenging. How can we continue to be vibrant, healthy, and "ageless," both inside and out, as time passes?

Being "ageless" isn't just about looking good (although we certainly will cover the physical aspects of aging), but to hold back the ravages of Father Time, we must go much further than "skin deep."

In this book, we will see how being ageless starts from within. We will look at and then go beyond the physical, mental, financial, and emotional levels, and then later explore the psychological and spiritual aspects of agelessness. You will begin to see "real beauty" in a whole new light.

Being ageless is not only about stopping the aging process on the outside, but also about discovering who you truly are on the inside. I do not believe you can have one without the other.

We will discuss all aspects of staying young. Superficial beauty IS only skin deep, but our true beauty is at the deepest level of our essence, and it endures. True beauty always survives. Let that "inner beauty" shine through, and it will keep you "ageless."

In *Ms. Ageless America*, we will disprove the "old wives' tale" that beauty is only skin deep. Instead, we will prove that true beauty goes all the way to the soul.

Chapter 1
NIGHT OF THE VAMPIRE

Everyone may think you're a vampire, but vampires don't get wrinkles and they stay young forever.

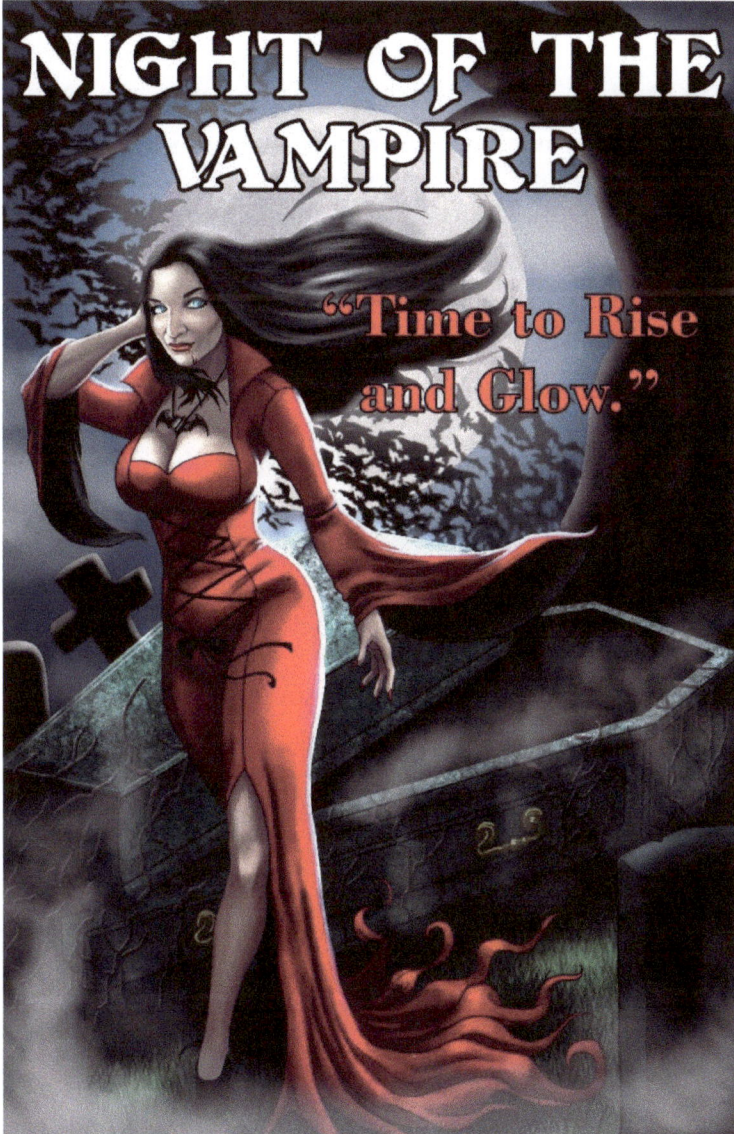

While your motivation may not be as strong as that of a vampire, in the long run you'll be glad you avoided the sun. Your older self will thank you. So if you don't want to have to go over to "the dark side" to stay young, stay out of the sun and get your "beauty sleep."

YOU MIGHT BE SURPRISED to learn that Dracula and your grandmother had something in common. They both know that the sun is bad for you. Very, very bad.

I know; I learned from my own early experience with sun exposure that the sun is not my friend. When I was a small child, my parents would take the whole family to the lake for the weekend. As the only one with curly bright red hair and very pale skin, it didn't take long for me to burn.

I'm afraid I had to learn my lesson the hard and rather painful way. Ever since, I've had an aversion to sunbathing, which I am thankful for because we now know how harmful the sun is for our skin.

What I used to think of as a curse has become more of a blessing. At my age, I am fortunate to have (of necessity) avoided years of sun exposure and skin damage.

In fact, exposure to the sun is probably the number one way to look older than your years. So if you've ever wondered how vampires look so good being hundreds of years old, now you know their secret to eternal youth and beauty. Avoid the sun at all costs. Maybe this is why vampires are immortal.

Ever since Bram Stoker introduced us to the tale of *Dracula* in 1897, we have been fascinated with stories about these immortal creatures. Who doesn't want to stay young and beautiful forever (without diet or exercise)? Just look at how some of our most alluring on-screen vampires – Winona Ryder in *Bram Stoker's Dracula*; Selma Hayek in

From Dust Until Dawn; Kate Beckinsale in *Underworld* and Rachelle LeFarre in *Twilight* – dazzle us with their seemingly eternal beauty and stoke our continued obsession with staying young.

DON'T BOW BEFORE THE SUN GODS

However, if you want to stay ageless, then you must, like all vampires, avoid the enticing lures of the sun gods and goddesses. Even though sun worship has been going on for centuries, don't be fooled by its empty promises of youth and beauty. Today we know better. So don't bow down to Sol, Surya, Akycha, Ekhi, Ra, Apollo or any of the ancient sun gods.

Leave sun worshipping (and premature skin aging) to the ancient Greeks and Romans. Ancient lore does say that vampires can be protected from the sun if they wear a Lapis Lazuli stone which has been forged by a witch, but I couldn't guarantee it. And it's hard to find a "good" witch when you need one.

Another reason most vampires avoid the sun? Perhaps after so many centuries, they find the soft glow of moonlight more flattering than the harsh rays of the sun. Maybe they have a point. Today the latest trend for anti-aging is a procedure called the "Vampire" facelift, which will be discussed later in the book.

THE NAKED TRUTH

Overexposure to the sun can not only give you wrinkles before your time, but the UV exposure can even lead to skin cancer. And you don't have to bake in the sun for this to happen; simply walking in and out of buildings during your daily routine, coaching your kid's soccer game, or even driving to work exposes you to those nasty ultraviolet rays. Have you ever noticed that your left arm — the one closest to the car window when you drive — often becomes pinker or darker than your right arm? Here are some facts from the Sun Safety Alliance[1] (an organization highly regarded by most vampires):

- Our children and grandchildren get three times more exposure to the sun than we do.
- Concrete, sand, water, and snow reflect almost 90 percent of the sun's UV rays (so there's no safe place to hide).
- Depletion of the Earth's ozone continues to increase our exposure to harmful UV rays.
- Surprisingly just one blistering sunburn can double the lifetime risk of developing skin cancer.

More than a million new cases of skin cancer are diagnosed each year in the United States. Melanoma, the deadliest form of skin cancer, kills one person every hour — and the majority of melanomas can be attributed to (you guessed it) – sun exposure.

100+ SPF OR PARASOL?
So what's a girl to do? Actually, it's not that difficult to protect yourself from the sun's harmful effects. In fact, back in the early years of the 20th century, women were diligent about protecting their skin from the sun's rays. High class ladies of that era wore hats and gloves and carried parasols. It was "in fashion" to be pale. But somewhere along about the middle of the 20th century, we forgot about the dangers of the sun and threw away our parasols. And at some point, a "suntan" look became fashionable in spite of the risks to our skin.

So, if you don't fancy walking around with a parasol like your grandmother did, or sleeping sunny days away in

[1] http://www.sunsafetyalliance.org/bare_facts.html

a coffin doesn't quite work for you, there are still plenty of things you can do to stave off the premature aging that sun damage brings.

The most important rule is to *wear sunblock of at least 15 SPF (30 for children) any time you are outdoors,* especially on sunny days or for prolonged periods of time. Remember that sunblock should be reapplied every couple of hours, and also after sweating very much, swimming or toweling off. There's no such thing as "waterproof" or "sweat proof" sunscreen. Don't miss those easy-to-forget places: lips, ears, neck and the tops of the feet, even the part in your hair, or all over the head for people with thinning hair.

For the best UV protection, look for products that provide broad spectrum protection, which screens against both UVB and UVA rays (these contain ingredients like Avobenzone [Parsol 1789] or zinc oxide).

Want additional protection from the "evil" sun?
Here are a few facts that every good vampire knows:

- Avoid being outdoors whenever possible between 10 am and 4 pm, when the sun is strongest.
- Dark clothing protects better than lighter fabrics.
- Wear sunglasses and a hat whenever possible in the sun (and, hey, that parasol or umbrella isn't a bad idea, either!).

What's the only thing worse for your skin than the sun? A tanning bed. NEVER use one if you want to stay looking young. Just 10 minutes in a tanning bed equates to an hour in the sun at the hottest part of the day.

Eventually your skin WILL show the effects of too much sun exposure. This shows up in sun spots, uneven skin tone, rough and cracked "alligator skin," those dreaded age-confirming wrinkles, or skin cancer, at its worst. At the very least, the results of too much sun will hinder your pursuit of looking young as you age.

JUST FAKE IT

Let's face it, though, there is something pretty and alluring (even if it isn't actually healthy for us) about that sun-kissed glow. If you feel you must have some semblance of a tan, go with one of the many excellent self-tanners available on the market. They've come a long way from the fake, streaky, orange lotions of the past. Today's top-notch products still come in lotion form, along with sprays and even wipes. The good ones are very natural looking, and build up color gradually, often while moisturizing the skin at the same time.

They often smell good as well, a huge improvement on that nasty odor, which is caused by dihydroxyacetone (DHA). DHA comes from plant sources such as beets and sugarcane, and their reaction to the amino acids in our skin is what adds the color and that tell-tale smell. But fortunately, the newer formulas use various ways to block or mask this scent.

THE LONG GOODNIGHT

Besides avoiding the sun, another one of Dracula's beauty secrets is his amazing ability to climb into his coffin, shut out the rest of the world and sleep the day away. Most of us mere mortals, however, simply do not get nearly enough sleep. Although I am unsure how many hours vampires actually sleep, that dusk-to-dawn period could range from eight to twelve hours, depending on the time of year.

By contrast, the average American only gets 6.8 hours of sleep per night — down from half a century ago. A recent

Gallup Poll[2] revealed that 40 percent of people in the U.S. get less than the recommended amount of sleep, which is seven to nine hours for adults. And we all know people who seem to exist on only four or five hours per night. I personally think that 10 to 12 hours is a better average, although maybe not possible for most people. And 14 percent of us are averaging five hours or less of snooze time per night.

More women than men report not getting enough sleep, and parents of young children are, not surprisingly, one of the most sleep-deprived groups.

A lack of adequate sleep has been related to all kinds of health problems such as high blood pressure, heart disease, and stroke, as well as low life satisfaction, stress, memory problems and cognitive impairment (you know, that fuzzy-headed feeling when you haven't had enough shut-eye).

According to the Division of Sleep Medicine at Harvard Medical School[3], sleep deprivation can also lead to other health problems, including obesity, diabetes, cardiovascular disease, and even early mortality.

All these things, along with posing serious health issues, can cause us to feel and look old before our time. Our bodies need time to repair and revitalize, and this is what sleep does for us. It's like a little daily vacation for our bodies. Our cells rejuvenate, the brain replaces chemicals and perhaps even solves problems while we sleep.

When Larell Scardelli asked her 92-year-old grandmother[4] how she stayed looking and feeling so young, her grandmother's answer was "…it's because I'm a good

---

[2] http://www.gallup.com/poll/166553/less-recommended-amount-sleep.aspx
[3] http://healthysleep.med.harvard.edu/healthy/matters/consequences
[4] https://www.goodhousekeeping.com/beauty/a20707202/old-fashioned-beauty-treatments/

sleeper." (More of grandma's beauty tips to follow in the next chapter).

So, if you want your skin and your body to look great at 60 or 90 — not to mention how you feel and your sharpness of mind — give it all a chance to recharge and renew. "Beauty sleep" isn't just a timeworn phrase — it really works!

And don't forget what Anne Rice's famous vampire Lestat de LionCourt (*The Vampire Chronicles*) says:

"None of us really changes over time. We only become more fully what we are."

This can be said for vampires and humans alike.

YOU MIGHT BE A VAMPIRE IF:

- ❖ You've never seen your reflection in a mirror
- ❖ Your periodontist has serious concerns about your bleeding gums
- ❖ You have a strong aversion to Italian food, especially with extra garlic
- ❖ You see nothing unusual about sleeping in a coffin
- ❖ You strongly prefer moonlight to sunlight
- ❖ Doesn't everyone sleep 12 hours a day (during the day)?
- ❖ All your friends have suddenly become very religious and are wearing crosses around their necks

Chapter 2
BEAUTY SECRETS OF THE AGES
Timeless Beauty Tips

LOGAN'S RUN

ENTER A WORLD WHERE everyone stays young forever. In the futuristic world of *Logan's Run*, all the residents are perpetually young, healthy and beautiful. No one looks a day over thirty. There is no sickness and no old age. The catch? Well, there IS no one over the age of 30.

At birth, a clear crystal is implanted in each newborn (who are raised by the "Nursery," not their mother). As the years pass, the crystal turns from clear to green to yellow then to red. When the crystal turns dark on the last day of your 29th year, everyone must try for "renewal."

That's when you have to take a ride on the "Carousel" to be renewed. For those NOT chosen for rejuvenation (which is everyone), when the merry-go-round stops, all the 29-year-old riders have been zapped and vaporized. They have passed on; moved to another dimension; entered the pearly gates or whatever euphemism you want to use. They are no longer of this world. They will never have to worry about wrinkles, weight, romance or finances.

Whatever we choose to call "death" unfortunately, it is the only proven way not to age. Most of us, however, are not too crazy about this option. We don't want to exit on the eve of our 30th birthday.

So just like "the runners" in *Logan's Run* who take off looking for Sanctuary as an alternative to their last carousel ride, we also try to escape our 30th, 50th, 60th, or 90th birthday party. We, too, keep searching for an alternative way to stay eternally young (without that annoying dying part).

THE SILVER SCREEN

While no one has actually found this "Sanctuary of Anti-aging," we can always look where images of beautiful women are frozen in time – on the Silver Screen.

In the 1920s, the emergence of the cosmetics industry within the motion picture industry created a phenomenon of glamour. Beauty became a cottage industry and quickly exploded in the United States. Before then the average housewife, teacher, or retail clerk did not use cosmetics. Makeup was used only by "women of the night."

But as images of beautiful women were splashed on the silver screen, the glamour of Hollywood was too much to resist. Now any woman (for a modest price) had access to that glamour through hair curlers, beauty masks, foundations, rouges, lipsticks and nail polishes.

Some of the most glamorous and beautiful women in America's history were from this era.

Here are just a few of these glamorous women who we will always think of as frozen in time and "forever young:"

- Grace Kelly
- Audrey Hepburn
- Marilyn Monroe
- Jacqueline Kennedy
- Elizabeth Taylor
- Ginger Rogers
- Lana Turner
- Lauren Bacall
- Katherine Hepburn
- Vivien Leigh
- Rita Hayworth
- Carole Lombard

- Jayne Russell
- Ava Gardner
- Jayne Mansfield
- Jean Harlow
- Susan Hayward
- Betty Grable
- Natalie Woods

Perhaps these women also knew beauty secrets we have forgotten today. Besides the new era of cosmetics available to them, there were also many natural beauty treatments and tips used during this time. These "secrets" can help keep the years away from our face and our body.

Many of these suggestions are preventive in nature, filled with good ole common sense, inexpensive and easily accessible. Most of the ingredients used can be found in your kitchen cabinets.

Here are some beauty tips that grandma, as well as stars of the Silver Screen, might have shared with us IF we had bothered to listen.

10 GRANDMA'S BEAUTY TIPS THAT WORK LIKE A CHARM:[5]

1. Wear gloves to protect your hands. Wear while driving or gardening or anytime to avoid sunspots. Wear when cleaning to avoid harsh chemicals or soapy water.
2. Cure skin breakouts with lemon. Mix lemon with water and apply. Lemon has antibacterial properties that will calm skin.

---

[5] https://www.beautyandtips.com/beauty-2/10-grandmas-beauty-tips-that-work-like-a-charm/

3. Exfoliate skin with sugar. Just add some sugar to your soap while bathing and watch those flaky dead skin cells flow down the drain.
4. Brush hair 100 times each night. This will stimulate hair follicles and give shine to your locks.
5. Use cocoa butter, shea butter or even lard as an overall body moisturizer. Also good for softening cuticles and wonderful as a lip balm.
6. Say bye-bye to under-eye dark circles with potatoes. If suffering from a late night and need a quick fix, cut a potato into pieces. Put a piece under each eye and wait about 10 minutes. Dark circles and puffiness will be much improved. (Also don't forget the old standby of warm tea bags. The caffeine in the tea will shrink blood vessels and gave your eyes a pick me up.)
7. Plump up those lips with cinnamon and beets. Mix some cinnamon with your shea butter and dab onto lips. This will increase the circulation around the mouth and give a fullness to the lips. Using beets might be a little more difficult, but I suppose you could just buy a stalk of beets to cut and rub onto your lips. Beets are excellent for circulation.
8. Lemon makes an excellent lightener. Squeeze it on your hair to get that sun-kissed look. You can either sit in the sun (with sunscreen) or use your hair dryer to let it lighten as it dries. Lemon is also an excellent way to lighten your fingernails and give you that French manicure look without the manicure.
9. Create a curly head of hair with strips of cloth. Instead of spending money and damaging your hair with harsh chemicals and/or heat, just rip some material (rags) into strips of cloth, roll wet hair and tie into a knot. After hair has dried, just take down your luscious locks. Actually, I just saw a Lori

Geiner "new" product very much like this idea. In the 1930s this was called "ragging."

10. Sleep on a silk pillowcase. Make sure you're not creating more wrinkles while you sleep. As you toss and turn at night, a softer material such as silk will not pull on your skin. Today there are even pillows that are hollow in the middle, so your face won't touch the pillow at all.

Here are still more words of beauty wisdom shared by many of our collective grandmothers:

- Go "singing in the rain" and rinse your hair with rainwater
- Rub cream from the top of fresh milk on your face
- Rhubarb is an excellent source of Vitamin C for your face
- Witch hazel will unclog pores and blackheads
- Use a whipped raw egg as a weekly facial mask
- Pour apple cider vinegar on hair once a week to give it shine
- Use coconut oil as a makeup remover
- Mayo isn't just for BLTs. Apply a large blob onto your locks to moisturize
- Mix oil, vinegar, salt and sugar to control breakouts

Also, don't leave honey out of your beauty regiment.[6] Honey can be applied directly to the face by itself to help moisturize and kill bacteria. You can also create a facial masque out of honey and yogurt (mix equal parts). Another excellent combination is honey and almonds. Just soak the almonds and mash them into a paste. Add honey and some

---

[6] https://www.goodhousekeeping.com/beauty/a20707202/old-fashioned-beauty-treatments/

lemon juice. Apply to face. Honey and water is also a great moisturizer for the hair.

Another excellent moisturizer and cleanser is goat's milk. Goat's milk has an excellent ph. value and will make your skin feel soft and supple.

And don't forget to exfoliate. As we age, our hormones decline causing the cellular turnover rate of our skin cells to decrease. So, it's important that we stimulate our skin to get rid of the top layers.

Inexpensive oatmeal soap is a wonderful way to exfoliate your face. You can even find oatmeal and honey combination soap, which will exfoliate and moisturize at the same time.

Another excellent skin exfoliator is papaya. Create a paste from the papaya and spread over face. The enzyme in the papaya will cause the cells in your skin to accelerate and create glowing skin underneath.

THINGS YOU WISH YOU COULD TELL YOUR GRANDMOTHER:

- ❖   I love you
- ❖   Oh, my God! You were right (about everything)
- ❖   I wished I'd never laid out in the sun
- ❖   That tattoo wasn't such a great idea after all
- ❖   And Billy Bob didn't make such a great husband, either
- ❖   Pretty IS as pretty does
- ❖   YOU should have been in the movies
- ❖   I wish you were here

Chapter 3
SMILE FOR THE CAMERA
It sure looks good on you.

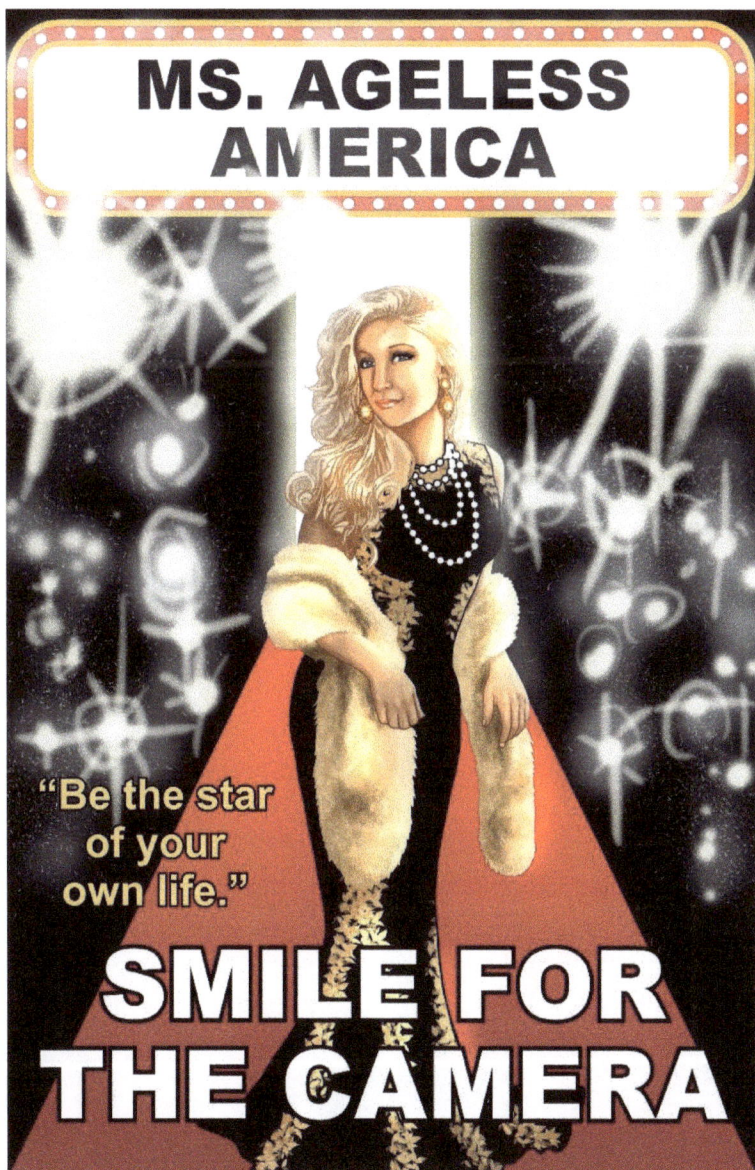

WHAT IS THE FIRST THING you notice when you meet someone new? Usually, it's the person's gender and race, according to Harvard researchers.[7] But after that, what strikes you most quickly? Their eyes, their smile, their hair? What they're wearing? Or perhaps a combination of these things?

Most people notice several attributes, though usually a predominant one immediately. Surveys show that it's about evenly split between smile and eyes, with 37 percent of people noticing a smile first, and 33 percent noticing the eyes first.[8] After that, 15 percent judge a person's weight, 9 percent the hair, and 2 percent the nose.

It is this combination of traits that makes each person unique. So, thinking about this, which description sounds like a younger person?

- Long, healthy, beautiful hair
- A dazzling smile with bright, white teeth
- Large, open eyes

OR

- Short, brittle, gray or unhealthy hair
- Yellowing teeth
- Hooded eyelids and/or bags under the eyes

Of course, we would all choose the first description as that of the youngest, healthiest person. But usually, as we age, features from the second description begin to make us appear older to others. Fortunately, there are many things

---

[7] http://news.harvard.edu/gazette/story/2013/10/whats-in-a-face/
[8] http://kymx.cbslocal.com/2012/11/15/the-first-thing-someone-notices-when-they-meet-you/

we can do to slow down, hide, or reverse these characteristics.

THE LONG AND SHORT OF IT

In our culture, generally it's assumed that when a woman reaches the age of around 40 – and most certainly by 50 – she should no longer have long hair. Short hairstyles are deemed more "appropriate" for women once we reach a certain age.

But personally, I have never seen someone who looked younger by cutting their hair shorter. In fact, I think that it has the opposite effect – shorter hair gives off the impression of maturity, while longer hair is (perhaps unconsciously) associated with youth, sexuality, and femininity.

Judith A. Waters, a psychology professor at Fairleigh Dickinson University, says that men's attraction to long hair on a woman is almost primeval:[9] "It used to be the one thing that distinguished women from men, at least from the back," she says.

Waters also suggests that men may find it less threatening, particularly in the workplace. "Longer hair can signal the men to not be nervous; 'boys, we're not after your jobs.' It`s a message of femininity and softness – a way of pacifying the enemy."

Of course, hairstyle is a completely personal choice, and there are good reasons why many women (of any age) choose to have shorter hair. But don't let anyone suggest that you "should" have shorter hair because of your age, or that having a shorter style is more "appropriate." Let them cut their own hair and grow old.

---

[9] http://articles.chicagotribune.com/1987-08-07/features/8702280087_1_hair-femininity-and-softness-psychologists

If your reason for keeping your hair short is concern about its thinning, there are many options today for women with thinning hair. Rogaine is showing promise for women; the company introduced a new 5 percent minoxidil formulation for women. It's a mousse (instead of a liquid) that needs to be applied only once a day instead of twice, which means that it can be more easily incorporated into a woman's evening skincare routine.

Products with keratin can make your hair thicker, and there are several supplements that are correlated with healthier hair (and nails), such as biotin and fish oil. There are several products on the market that are specifically for hair growth or improvement, though their results are inconsistent. Some women take prenatal vitamins, even when they aren't pregnant, because of its often-beneficial results in the hair.

I have even seen special LED type brushes and caps advertised that are supposed to encourage hair growth.

I would think that any type of routine that stimulates the hair follicles would be beneficial.

More extreme (and costly) hair thickening options include laser treatment and a new procedure called Platelet Rich Plasma (PRP), which uses the person's own blood plasma in the scalp via injection. And new research is being done on hair follicle stem cells to create new hair.[10]

Of course, the longer you allow your hair to grow, the more important it is that it stays healthy. When you aren't cutting the ends off regularly, they can become much drier and brittle. Even if you're growing or maintaining long hair, slightly trimming the dead ends regularly is important.

Deep condition your locks at least once a week. An easy, inexpensive, and natural way to condition and thicken hair is

---

[10] https://www.nytimes.com/2015/04/16/fashion/new-hair-thinning-treatments-for-women.html?_r=0

to have what I call a "happy hour" in the shower. After washing your hair, simply pour a can of beer all over your wet head. Don't wash it out, just leave it in and dry as usual.

After it dries, amazingly there is no beer smell at all, just bouncy and conditioned hair. And yes, any brand will do – just grab whatever is in the fridge or on sale at the local grocery. Many women also swear by coconut oil to naturally deep condition and nourish hair. Argan oil has also received attention, particularly for women of color. Any oils should be rinsed out of hair after they've been left on for a while.

TO COLOR OR NOT TO COLOR

When it comes to coloring your hair or letting it go gray naturally, that also is entirely up to each person. I've seen women with a thick head of white, silver, or gray hair who look amazing. It's also become an incredibly popular trend among young people, in their teens to thirties, to dye their hair a silver or gray color – taking away much of the stigma of the color being reserved only for older folks.

However, it is a little trickier to look young with gray hair, when you aren't 20 or 30. Women with dark hair will have to address this issue sooner than those with blonde or red hair. Gray strands are much more prominent in darker hair, so consider addressing this issue as soon as "salt and pepper" starts to appear.

Often, women with lighter hair can get away with it longer as the gray strands begin to appear; blondes particularly often turn more silver than gray, and the strands can look like highlights before they begin to be very prevalent. I call this "blonding" instead of graying.

If gray isn't your choice, keeping your natural color – or changing to something else entirely – is easy these days. You can do it yourself with a rinse or coloring kit from your local beauty supply or drugstore. Many of today's products are not nearly as harsh and damaging as the hair dye of old, and many even have ingredients that soften and condition your strands. However, there have been recent studies that suggest women who regularly color their hair may have a greater chance of developing cancer, so you might want to stay with natural products.

If you're going to color your hair, and are staying with your natural color, you might want to go a shade lighter. Very dark hair can emphasize wrinkles or look harsher, so a bit of brightening or highlights can counter this. There are options for lightening hair from kits and professional salon highlighting to home remedies that include lemon juice, vinegar, hydrogen peroxide, honey and chamomile.

If you have dark hair and want to hide the gray naturally when it begins to appear, try a coffee or tea rinse. Tints made from herbs are also a great natural choice, and home remedies often include henna, and beet or carrot juice (especially for red locks). There's even a natural hair color product called Herbatint which uses herbs to "dye" your hair.

A DAZZLING SMILE

Everyone wants a bright, white smile. As we age, our smiles begin to fade and teeth turn yellow, naturally, and from things like smoking and drinking coffee or tea. But today, just like with your hair color, achieving or maintaining a brilliant smile is easy and generally inexpensive (although there are costlier options, such as veneers).

Not too long ago when the whitening craze hit, people had to spend hundreds of dollars at the dentist for the procedure. Now, there are many over-the-counter products that can be just as effective if used properly and consistently. Whitening strips, gels, toothpaste, and light pens can all do the trick. You can also buy mouth trays over the counter or go ahead and see your dentist about them.

Doing it yourself may take a little longer than a professional treatment, but if you keep at it, you can still get great results at a fraction of the cost. So, stay young, and give yourself a reason to keep smiling!

THE EYES HAVE IT

We've all heard the phrase, "The eyes are the window to the soul."

When you first meet someone, their eyes are typically one of the first things you notice. Whether they are the window to the soul or not is debatable; however, they are often a tell-tale giveaway to one's age.

Crow's feet, bags, dark circles and puffiness indicate someone has had a lot of life experience. And we've all seen people with the dreaded "11" lines between their eyes. How to avoid these nasty little aging signs without plastic surgery?

First, try to break the habit of wrinkling your forehead and/or squinting your eyes in concentration. Also, a smile creates far less wrinkles than a frown, both around the mouth and in the forehead.

As your mother likely told you: "Don't make a face like that, or it will freeze that way." She may just have been right. Continued facial movements will affect your facial muscles. So, let's make sure it's for the better.

In Chapter 5, I share facial exercises that are specifically meant for keeping the eye area wrinkle-free and open. If more than these natural fixes are needed, some of the possibilities include:

- Subdermal fillers such as Restylane, collagen, fat, and of course, Botox. (We will discuss these dermal fillers in much greater detail later in the book).
- Over-the-counter products to temporarily smooth and tighten skin around the eyes. These range from

inexpensive – under $20 – to very expensive – $500
or more. You cannot use makeup immediately after
applying the product as it will crease, effectively
creating more wrinkles.

But beware! Many people have unpleasant reactions to
these treatments. I, personally, wouldn't want to risk the
potential side effects. I still want to be able to smile and
make facial expressions. I'm not a big fan of going through
life looking continually and mildly surprised. I also want to
avoid those puckered "fish" lips and "cat" eyes that
injections can give.

Keep your long, sexy mane, your dazzling smile, and
your soulful "real" eyes, and no one will ever guess your
true age. Then toss your head back, run your fingers
through your silky hair, show those pearly whites, open up
those eyes and wink at the younger guy sitting next to you.

But I assume no responsibility for what happens next.

YOU MIGHT THINK YOU'RE A STAR IF:
- ❖ You think you see paparazzi every time you take out the trash.
- ❖ When the waiter brings you your bill, you think he's asking for your autograph.
- ❖ You're sure you have a greater vocal range than Celine Dion.
- ❖ You won't use "the facilities" unless they've been supplied with fresh flowers.
- ❖ You have more feather boas than Cher.

Chapter 4
RED, RED WINE

Wine a little bit-you'll feel better.

ANOTHER THING THAT gives our age away is our weight. As the years pass, we tend to put on a few extra pounds here and there. While a few pounds won't affect how young you look, too many pounds will. Most people can put on 10 pounds or so without affecting how young they look, but when we start to get 20 or 30 pounds plus heavier it can change our appearance drastically and make us look older.

It is very easy to put on a pound a year, and most of us do. But if you want to fit into that favorite little black dress and wow your classmates and old rivals at your 30-year high school reunion, it's a good idea to watch what and how much you eat. It's a lot easier to not gain the weight in the first place than it is to take the weight off later.

How do you do that? First, eat smaller portions. Micro-size your meals instead of super-sizing them. Our American culture promotes an unhealthy amount of food in one meal. Split a meal with a friend or just eat half. If you're cooking at home, cook smaller portions.

Second, eat slowly. Give your body a chance to realize it's full before you stuff more food into your body. It takes the body and the brain a while (about 20 minutes) to realize it's full and to register that it's had enough. So give it time. Let your brain talk to your stomach.

Third, avoid mindless eating. Watch what you eat. And watch when you eat it. Often, we eat just because we're bored or nervous or depressed. Don't do it. Find another way to deal with life's ups and downs.

H20

Another way to trick your body into thinking it's full is to drink lots and lots of water. In fact, you should drink half of your weight in water (in ounces) daily. So, if you weigh 130 pounds, it's a good idea to drink 65 ounces (four 16-ounce bottles) of water every day. Instead of drinking that Diet

Coke with unhealthy aspartame, grab a bottle of water. Your body will thank you for it.

RED WINE

If you're looking for something a little stronger to drink at that high school reunion-and we all know how stressful it can be running into frenemy Suzie after all these years-try a glass of red wine. The resveratrol in red wine has proven to be an excellent anti-aging factor. Of course, to get the full benefit, you might want to try getting some of your resveratrol in capsules instead of getting all its benefits in liquid form.

APPLE CIDER VINEGAR

Another excellent drink to add to your diet is apple cider vinegar. It should be organic. Braggs is excellent and probably the most popular brand. This miracle drink will help reduce your appetite, control blood sugar spikes, and will also help with weight loss. It is also an excellent natural laxative. Just be sure not to drink it straight or it will burn your esophagus. Add one tablespoon of apple cider vinegar to an eight-ounce glass of water. Drink at least once a day. Twice a day is even better.

MEDITERRANEAN DIET

If you really want to stay looking young, healthy, and thin, it's probably best not to eat the average American diet. Almost two-thirds of Americans are overweight, and that number is only likely to increase. So, if you want to avoid being part of that statistic, stop eating like an American and start eating like you're in the Mediterranean.

What does the Mediterranean diet have that Americans don't? It's mostly what it DOESN'T have and it's what they DON'T eat. The modern American diet consists largely of highly processed food made with genetically modified grains – grains laced with chemical additives. Our wheat, which used to contain about 10 percent gluten, now has up to 30 percent gluten. This is not the same wheat our parents and grandparents used to eat. And if you look at their photos, even if they're in black and white, and not smiling, they probably were not overweight.

Our food in America has changed, and not for the better. So, we have to be proactive and take our health and our looks into our own hands. No one else will. Eat whole, unprocessed food as often as possible. Avoid a lot of heavy sauces, breads, and desserts. If you must have a certain food, eat just a few bites instead of the whole thing.

Have you ever noticed that the first bite of whatever it is always tastes the best? Eat slowly and savor your favorite foods. Don't try to avoid certain foods completely, though (say Krispy Kreme donuts or chocolate cake). I have found if I say I cannot eat something it just makes me want it more and I end up sitting with powdered sugar all over me looking guilty (after I've devoured half a dozen Krispy Kremes). Just give yourself permission to eat a donut slowly, maybe once a week, as a reward.

The Mediterranean diet consists of much more natural, unprocessed foods. Olive oil, fresh fruits, and vegetables, which are much healthier for your heart and your waistline.

There are even more radical diet ideas. For example, Carol Alt, famous supermodel, eats only raw food. I would imagine it would be a bit tricky to order in a restaurant, but she is totally thin, healthy, and gorgeous at age 56.

WEIGHT LOSS PROGRAMS
So, what to do if you've already put on some of those unwanted extra pounds?

If you're finding it too difficult to take the weight off on your own, you might want to try one of the many commercial weight loss programs. Today there are a myriad of them to choose from so I did a little research trying to determine the best ones. Here's what I found.

The Daily Meal.com looked at 12 of the best and worst commercial weight loss programs.[11] An expert panel of doctors, nutritionists, nurses, and clinicians evaluated the various programs and here's how they rated them from WORST to BEST:

- WonderSlim – Worst
- Flat Belly diet
- LA Weight Loss
- Biggest Loser Diet
- Medifast
- Curves Complete
- Atkins
- Nutrisystem
- Jenny Craig
- DASH for Health
- South Beach Diet
- Weight Watchers – Best

Of all these programs, Weight Watchers was overwhelmingly voted the most effective for weight loss and the most supportive of a healthy lifestyle.

The experts said it was the best at showing people "how to think about quality and quantity of food so that they can initiate and maintain weight loss."

In another survey done by U.S. News.com, Weight Watchers was also found to be the best program for weight loss. Jenny Craig and Volumetrics tied for second place.

HMR diet was number three while the Raw Food Diet and the Biggest Loser Diet tied for fifth place.

---

[11] https://www.thedailymeal.com/12-best-and-worst-weight-loss-programs-according-experts/51414

Weight Watchers has also sponsored their own study, conducted by Baylor College of Medicine.[12] In this study they found that people were eight times more likely to lose 5 percent of their body weight and nearly nine times more likely to lose 10 percent of their body weight after six months of participating in Weight Watchers compared to those who participated only in self-help groups. This resulted in the Weight Watchers group losing a total average of 10 pounds while the self-help group lost less than a pound and a half.

In another study,[13] several commercial weight loss programs were examined including Slimfast, Medifast, Health Management Resources (HMR), CoolSculpt, Optifast, Atkins, Biggest Loser Club, eDiets, Lose It!, Weight Watchers, Jenny Craig and NutriSystem.

In this study Jenny Craig came out on top as the best program.

Of all these weight loss programs only Jenny Craig and Weight Watchers achieved any significant weight loss that was sustained for at least 12 months.

Almost 5 percent of participants lost and maintained weight loss with Jenny Craig and about half as many (2.6 percent) with Weight Watchers were able to lose more weight than people dieting on their own.

NutriSystem participants also showed a 3.8 percent greater weight loss than people not enrolled in the program. However, this was only for a three-month period and there were no long term results.

If you're on a diet, you're not alone. On any given day it's estimated that 50 million Americans are on some type of diet. But don't let it define who you are. Watching what you

---

[12] https://www.huffpost.com/entry/weight-watchers-study-self-help_n_4099023

[13] https://www.livescience.com/50394-weight-loss-programs-effective.html

eat is fine, but don't be too critical of yourself. Accept yourself just as you are and visualize yourself at your desired weight. See yourself as that skinny person. Eat healthy food and eat appropriate portions. And if you just can't lose that last extra 10 pounds, don't despair. Having a little extra weight helps give your face a younger, fuller, and plumper appearance, something we want and need as we age.

Next, find an exercise program that you truly enjoy, not something you dread. (We will be discussing this more in detail in the next chapter.)

SUPPLEMENTS

Another excellent way to fight aging is to take supplements. As we age, our skin gets thinner, drier, and less elastic, which leads to wrinkles. But probiotics can help us fight back.

Lactobacillus plantarum and hy7714 probiotics have been shown to decrease wrinkles and improve skin elasticity. So besides helping your digestion, probiotics can help you look younger. Other supplements for anti-aging (according to Prevention magazine):

- Polypodium leucotomos extract from Central American farms help to preserve human skin's hypoblast. Hypoblast builds and restores collagen to help sagging skin and wrinkles. You can take 500 milligrams a day.
- Vitamin C can be taken orally and topically, and is shown to decrease oxidative stress in cells. Helps build, regenerate, and produce healthier skin, healthier and more vibrant skin. At least 100 milligrams a day.
- Vitamin E has antioxidants and anti-inflammatory capabilities, which helps skin regenerate and keeps

skin more radiant and faster cell turnover. 200 milligrams a day.

- Glucosamine taken both topically and orally, according to *The Journal of Dermatologic Treatment,* shows dramatic reduction in visible wrinkles and fine lines from oral ingestion. 1500 milligrams a day. According to *The Journal of Cosmetic Dermatology,* glucosamine as a supplement results in improved skin hydration and decreased in wrinkles. Glucosamine works with hyaluronic acid, which plumps the skin.

- CoQ10 helps overall appearance of the skin. In a Japanese trial, women who took CoQ10 orally showed a reduction in appearance of wrinkles after just two weeks. And it's 200 milligrams a day.

- Astaxanthin is another supplement that can be beneficial in keeping your skin looking young. Astaxanthin can help protect you against the effects of the sun's harmful ultraviolet rays, which can cause your skin to lose its elasticity. These rays also cause dryness, wrinkles, and sagging skin. A study published in the *Journal of Clinical Biochemistry and Nutrition,*[14] of 65 women ranging in age from 35 to 60 found that the women in the placebo group (not taking astaxanthin) had increased wrinkles and less moisture in their skin after a four-month period. However, those women who had taken at least 6 mg or as much as 12 mg of astaxanthin daily showed no symptoms of continued deterioration from sun exposure.

- Coffee Berry isn't only good for your morning jolt to get you out of bed. It is also good for your skin. It

---

[14] https://www.ncbi.nlm.nih.gov/pmc/articles/PMC5525019/

will help improve the appearance of fine lines and wrinkles.

So, gather those bottles of water around you, swallow your probiotics, your astaxanthin and your CoQ10, limit your Krispy Kremes and eat a big juicy apple. Then grab your bottle of red wine and pretend you're in the Greek Isles lying on the beach (with SPF protection, of course) and frenemy Suzie from high school is not invited.

YOU MIGHT HAVE HAD ENOUGH WINE IF:
- ❖ Your favorite liquor store sends you a birthday card every year
- ❖ ALL the liquor stores in town send you a birthday card every year
- ❖ Your favorite liquor store sends the cops for a "wellness check" when they haven't seen you in 48 hours
- ❖ You get a bill from the local police station for overtime when ALL the liquor stores in town simultaneously make the same request to check in on you
- ❖ You really prefer red wine to milk with your morning Cap'n Crunch

Chapter 5
GET ON UP, LET'S DANCE!
Oh, Oh, Oh, Listen To the Music

AMERICA HAS BECOME a country of couch potatoes. If we're not sitting in front of our computer, we're sitting in front of our television. It's a lifestyle that has evolved in the last decade and is a very hard habit for most of us to break. That is why our children and grandchildren are becoming overweight at younger and younger ages. Recess and physical education are a thing of the past. But if we want to keep ourselves and the next generation healthy, young, and vibrant, some lifestyle changes have to be made.

If you're over the age of 40, you know it's hard enough to keep the weight off as each day passes. Remember in Chapter 3 we said the average person gains at least a pound a year. But if our children and grandchildren are already overweight in their adolescence, it's very unlikely that they will be thin and healthy as they age.

What can we, as a nation, do to stay young and be healthy? Whether we are 7 or 70, we can start moving. It doesn't have to be an elaborate exercise program. Just do something. Something almost anyone can do at any age is walk. Just a 10 or 15 minute walk a day can make a difference. Walk outside, walk inside, walk around the mall, walk on a treadmill, or walk up the stairs instead of taking the elevator. How many calories can you burn walking? You can burn up to 100 calories for every mile you walk.

What if you can't walk? Then start by doing stretches. Stretches can be done just sitting in a chair or even lying down. I do leg and back stretches each morning before even getting out of bed. From stretches, you can move to Pilates and yoga. Yoga is great for both body and mind. Also, there are plenty of free weights and exercise machines that target specific areas of the body.

Running is another type of exercise that many people enjoy. That runner's high comes from endorphins. Yes, exercise not only keeps you thinner, it also helps you feel better, too.

However you do it, it's important to get your heart rate up. This increases your blood flow and burns off the calories. Studies show that individuals who do some kind of exercise that gets the heart rate up live longer, are fitter and thinner, have overall better health, have less chronic disease, and are even happier.

According to *NPR*,[15] women who walked on a regular basis in their fifties were much healthier in their later years. However, a word of caution about running, it can be very hard on your joints and your knees, so everything in moderation. Don't overdo and create other physical problems. You don't have to start out by running the Boston Marathon.

Swimming. If walking, running, or strenuous physical exercise is not really your thing, you might consider swimming. Swimming is easy on your joints and your knees. It's an excellent and enjoyable way to stay in shape. You can exercise your entire body all at once. Every muscle group is utilized while swimming. Both upper and lower body are working at the same time. Swimming also helps lower stress, strengthen bones, and improve flexibility, and in just 10 minutes you can burn up to 100 calories.

While you're at the gym, whether swimming or weightlifting, don't bypass the steam room and the sauna. This is my favorite part of the workout. Besides being totally relaxing as your muscles just let go, visiting the

---

[15] https://www.npr.org/sections/health-shots/2010/01/women_and_walking_the_benefits.html

steam room and sauna is an excellent way to get rid of toxins that have built up in your body all week. Don't ignore this. Also, the sauna can "temporarily" help you lose weight. I've been in the sauna with high school wrestlers who had to qualify for their weight class the next day. They say it works and you can lose as much as five pounds before weigh in. Of course, please do drink plenty of water while in the sauna. Staying in the sauna too long can make you very light-headed. Build up slowly, five minutes at a time. I like to stay at least half an hour in the sauna, but always drink plenty of water. When my water runs out, I leave. Go at your own pace. Sometimes the sauna is the only "exercise" I do, but I feel great; I've sweated out toxins and gotten my heart rate up.

Facial exercises. We often focus on building muscles and exercising our bodies but neglect our facial muscles. Yes, you can exercise your facial muscles just as your other muscles to help you keep looking younger. Suzanne Sommers, and now others, are promoting facial exercise machines. FaceMaster and other devices are available for reasonable prices. However, some of these exercises can be performed without any devices, just by looking in the mirror. Actually, the best facial exercise is smiling. When you smile, all your muscles are tightening and going in an upward direction, thereby tightening, and firming your face.

Other facial exercises:

- To banish under eye bags and firm up eye muscles, flex the muscles under your eyes, slightly squint, hold for five seconds, and then let go. Repeat 10 times. This will smooth out under eye bags and wrinkles.
- To rid yourself of marionette lines, and strengthen jaw muscles, curl your lower lip over your bottom

teeth, stick your chin out, hold for five seconds, and repeat 10 times. There are actually several websites showing you how to do facial exercises or face yoga. So smile and don't forget your face while exercising.

If you really want to have fun with your exercise, try dancing. Apparently, researchers have found that dancing can also have an anti-aging effect on your health. Dancing seems to stimulate the hippocampus, which controls memory, learning and balance.

In a study published in *Frontiers in Human Neuroscience*,[16] 26 people with a mean age of 86 were monitored for 18 months. One group learned dance routines while the other group performed endurance and flexibility exercises.

Both groups showed an increased and improved hippocampus volume, but the group that danced also showed a significant increase in the balance portion of the testing.

So, stimulate your brain and your body at the same time. Just pick something that makes you want to get up out of your chair, whether it's Zumba, Golden Oldies, Disco, Clogging or Square Dancing. Or make up your own dance moves.

You might want to stick with music from the past. Today's techno is a little more difficult to dance/exercise to. We're not looking to just stand in one place twitching and jerking like an unsuspecting epileptic in the throes of a convulsion.

The '70s and '80s produced some good dance music (exercise music), such as Michael Jackson's *Thriller*, *Black or White*, *Don't Stop Till You Get Enough*. *Bad Girls* by Donna Summers, or *Shake Your Groove Thing* by Peaches and Herb.

---

[16] https://www.frontiersin.org/articles/10.3389/fnhum.2017.00305/full

Or go even further back and pull out some Motown music. There you'll find serious rhythm to get your body moving. Marvin Gay's *Heard It Through the Grapevine*. *Can't Get Enough of Your Love* by Barry White, Lionel Richie's *All Night Long*. Commodore's *Brick House* and Diana Ross' *Upside Down*. Just pick your favorite kind of music, turn up the volume, and boogie down.

I, for one, can't sit still when I hear anything by the Doobie Brothers, and anything disco. Pick your favorite dance, have fun, improve your balance, and watch the pounds start to fade away. You won't even realize you're exercising. As the great James Brown said, "Get on up. Let's dance."

YOU MIGHT NEED MORE EXERCISE IF:

- ❖ Your idea of a marathon is shuffling from the bedroom to the kitchen and back
- ❖ Your couch has an imprint of your derriere (and you just bought the couch six weeks ago)
- ❖ It takes you 45 minutes to blow out your birthday candles
- ❖ You're building up your arm muscles by doing curls with your wine glass (lifting it to your mouth as many times as possible).
- ❖ The last time you went out dancing, everyone was doing the Charleston.

Chapter 6
YOU WEAR IT WELL
Mirror, Mirror:
Who's the Prettiest One of All?

WHAT DO YOU SEE when you look in the mirror? Someone who is vibrant, happy, youthful, or someone else? Who you really are is inside of you, sure, but don't you want that person to show on the outside, too? How can your self-image of youthfulness be the same one that others see?

We've already discussed how eyes, teeth, hair, skin, and weight can give away your age. So, say you've avoided the pitfalls of an unfortunate hairstyle, bags under eyes, wrinkles caused by too much sun, brittle gray hair, and too many pounds. You're looking in the mirror and you see healthy, bouncy, shiny hair, whether it's blonde, red, black, brown, or silver, and white teeth and wide-open eyes and few, if any, wrinkles, and a healthy waist size.

Okay, you're ready to go, right?

Well, not exactly. Where DID you get that dress or that top or those pants? If it wasn't in this century, you might have a little more work to do. You know what I'm talking about. You've seen the makeover shows on TV where some poor, unsuspecting, middle-aged lady is ambushed, kidnapped, and shamed into a new wardrobe and a new style. Sometimes the results aren't too bad; sometimes the new look is totally inappropriate; usually it looks as if someone is trying to make them look younger or hipper (like your granddaughter dressed you for the evening with her clothes).

So, if you don't want the style police showing up at your door and whisking you away to save you from yourself and your outdated closet, it's probably best to be proactive. It's time to create your own style. Don't let anyone else tell you what that might be. You are the only one who knows and the only one who matters. It must be what you are comfortable with. It's fine to get opinions from that granddaughter, neighbor, sister, or your husband, but you have the final say in what you want your style to be.

If every day is sweatpants and t-shirts for you, then own it. If you want to be a Renaissance lady and wear long, flowing dresses every day, then go for it. If you're an FBI agent want-to-be, wear those black pants, white shirt, and black leather jacket.

Whatever you choose, just know it's your decision. But please don't think that it doesn't matter what you wear, that nobody notices your clothes, your shoes, your jewelry. People do notice. In fact, experiments show that more attractive and better dressed people are treated, well, better.

What is considered more attractive? Universally speaking, for women, it's high cheekbones, fuller lips, big eyes, and thin chin. It's a little different for men. People prefer men to have a big jaw and a broad chin. Other beauty pluses include smooth skin, shiny hair, and facial symmetry. If you have these beauty factors, the world will reward you handsomely.

According to an article from *Business Insider*,[17] life is better if you're beautiful. You're not only prettier, but you're also considered smarter and are more likely to be wealthy and healthy.

As Keith Morrison discovered in his Dateline hidden camera investigation, *Do Looks Really Matter?*[18] the answer was an unequivocal "yes." The more attractive individuals, whether male or female, were given much more attention and assistance than the average Joe or Judy. Whether asking for directions, helping to pick up stray papers, or even just asking for change for a dollar, the more attractive people were treated better 100 percent of the time.

---

[17] https://www.businessinsider.com/science-backed-reasons-life-is-better-if-youre-beautiful-2015-12

[18] http://www.nbcnews.com/id/3917414/ns/dateline_nbc/t/face-value/#.XAm5H-JRe70

So, if you want help with directions, better service in a restaurant, quicker seating at an event, more fawning in the department store (Julia Roberts in *Pretty Woman*), getting bumped to the front of the line, or even that next promotion or raise, then dress for success. Make yourself one of the attractive people.

Here are a few tips for selecting your wardrobe. First, last, and always, be yourself and be comfortable. If you want to look thinner, try these tips:

- Stay with monochromatic colors. Of course, dark colors such as black are best, but if you don't want to wear black all the time (fear of being mistaken for a ninja) even all turquoise or all yellow or all blue will get the same effect as solid black, just not as dramatic.
- Also, solid colors, or at least minimal patterns, are preferable to large prints or florals. Large patterns of any kind will always make you look larger. You can always add a colorful printed scarf.
- Please, please avoid horizontal stripes. Yes, they will make you look larger. If you want to do stripes, go vertical.
- Don't go too short in dress length.
- If you go with a maxi dress, wear as high a heel as is comfortable. Every inch can hide/disguise 10 pounds.
- Yes, women over 60 *can* wear yoga pants in spite of what "what's his name" said.

And these are all just suggestions. If you're a big fan of horizontal stripes, far be it from me to tell you that you are wrong. As I said, your style is YOUR style and your business. Just find it, flaunt it, and stick with it.

So now when you look in that mirror and say, "Who's the prettiest one of all?" you'll know the answer. You are.

IT MIGHT BE TIME FOR A MAKEOVER IF:

- ❖ Your college sorority prom was the last time you went shopping for a new dress.
- ❖ The ladies at the Goodwill store offer you free clothes when you walk in.
- ❖ Strangers keep asking where you got your outfit, then laugh (about what, you don't know)
- ❖ Most of your wardrobe was purchased in the last century.
- ❖ You think khakis are a bold fashion statement.

Chapter 7
GO YOUR OWN WAY
There is only one you

HAVE YOU SEEN the perfume commercial where Julia Roberts walks into a black-tie gala ball? Everyone else is wearing black. She walks in in a white dress, and everyone looks at her like there is something wrong with her. But she ignores them and "breaks the bonds" that are holding her back and becomes her own unique person. She even frees everyone else in the room.

This commercial could be about much more than perfume.

The Lancôme perfume is "La Vie Est Belle," which in French means "Life is Beautiful."

Lancôme describes the perfume as "a choice embraced by women, not an imposed standard. The choice to live one's life and fill it with beauty." Your own way.

I'm not exactly sure that a perfume can do all that, but it is certainly a nice sentiment. It's an example of an awakened life and going your own way.

Have you ever felt like that? Like you are the one who just doesn't quite fit in with the rest of the crowd? Maybe you've even thought there was something wrong with you because you didn't look, talk, and act like everyone else.

As a child I know I had numerous "opportunities" to feel this way. When I was about five years old, my pale blonde hair suddenly started to turn a bright red. It didn't take long for "I'd rather be dead than red on the head" chants to become part of my daily routine. Then in the 5th grade, I hit an early growth spurt, standing head and shoulders above all my classmates. Soon the phrase "granddaddy long legs" was added to the repertoire. They weren't being mean; children just say it like it is. But no child wants to stand out, to be different.

But I learned (through the years) to accept these differences. At a young age, I learned it is ok to be different. I have learned to embrace my hair color, my height, and all the other things that make me who I am. And what other people think of you is often not even up to you. As Wayne Dyer said in one of his many wonderful books, "It's really none of my business what someone else's opinion of me is." That line has stayed with me ever since I first read it.

Sometimes we can go through life thinking we are out of place, out of time, we just don't fit in. Well, if you're one of those "misplaced" people, congratulations. As Socrates said, "the unexamined life is not worth living."

How do you know if your life is examined, unexamined, or not? Well, you have to examine it first to find out. You have to really take a good long look at it. Instead of just mindlessly going through the motions, ask yourself, *What am I doing with my life? Is this really what I want my life to be?*

If you are evolved enough to do that, then you have examined your life. The trick is that you can't un-examine it. You can't go back to blissful not knowing. It's like finding out the earth is round instead of flat. You can't "unknown" it.

But why would you want to? Yes, it might be easier to just go along with the crowd, never having to think for yourself, but is that what you really want for yourself? Each and every one of us is special. There is no one else in the world exactly like you. You were given unique gifts and talents that are yours alone. They were given to you to use and develop, and then give back to the world. Don't hide who you are, your unique talents, just because you're embarrassed or unsure of yourself or think you should be like everyone else. We were not meant to all be the same. Can you imagine how boring that would be? Embrace your uniqueness. Let others see what makes you the special person you are. As Margaret Mead said, "Always remember that you are absolutely unique. Just like everyone else."

YOU MIGHT NOT BE LIVING AN EXAMINED LIFE IF:
- ❖ You always agree with everyone else.
- ❖ Everyone always agrees with you.
- ❖ You ALWAYS do what you're told.
- ❖ You ask someone else what your opinion is.
- ❖ You know you are always right.

Chapter 8
DREAM ON
Following Your Dreams Will Keep You Young

HOW DO YOU KNOW who that special person inside of you is? How do you know which road to take? You make a choice. Sure, you can get other people's opinions and advice, but the final decision is always yours. How can you be sure you'll make the best decision? You can't. You just have to go for it. There is no guarantee in life. And we don't always get it right the first time. I don't know about you, but I usually get it wrong the first time. I make a mistake first. And that is the best way to learn anything; finding out how NOT to do something. Remember as a child learning how to ride a bicycle? I know I kept falling and scraping my knees before I got it right. And I'm betting you did, too.

Sure, there are a few people who get everything right the first time. But most of us have to learn the hard way, by making mistakes. But don't become afraid of finding your way because it's painful, either physically or emotionally. Don't be one of those people who's afraid to try because they might make a mistake. If you get to the end of your life without making a mistake, you haven't really lived at all.

Don't stay on the main path all your life; find your own way. It may not be easy but forging your own path will be much more fulfilling and satisfying. Yes, you can fall, and it can hurt. A lot. But when you were a child trying to ride that bicycle, did you give up the first time you fell? Or the second? Or the third? Probably not. You were going to learn how to ride that bike. So why is it we, as adults, won't take that chance? We think it better not to try at all. We might fail. And if we do try and fail, we certainly never try again.

Why is it ok for us to try and fail when we are 10, but not when we're 30 or 60 or even 80? Don't quit trying.

Life has a knack of getting in the way of our dreams: you get pregnant, go bankrupt, get divorced, get fired, win the lottery, fall down the stairs, fall up the stairs, buy a big new house, break your ankle, break someone else's finger, lose a talent contest, win a beauty pageant, blow all the money you won in the lottery, your brother gets married, you're in a movie, your sister dies, you get a new job in a new city, your neighbor has cancer, then she gets well, and then out of nowhere you win the lottery again!

Oh, and you get to watch the total eclipse of the sun!

How can you be expected to even remember what your goals are, much less reach them and fulfill your dreams with all this (life) constantly going on?

As the paper towel commercial so wisely tells us, "Life Gets Messy." And it does. The only thing predictable about life is that it is unpredictable.

Some days are awesome, and some are awful. The awesome ones seem to go by quickly. The other ones, not so fast.

No, life isn't perfect. Not yours, not mine, not anyone's. But don't give up on it. Don't ever be that person who says, "I wished I had…"

Many people don't fulfill their dreams until they are in their sixties or seventies.

Anna Mary Robertson Moses – "Grandma Moses" – didn't begin painting as a career until she was 78 years old. Some of her paintings went on to sell for more than a million dollars each.

If you've ever watched *Little House on the Prairie*, then you've heard of Laura Ingalls Wilder. She was 65 when she published her first book, *Little House in the Big Woods*. She was 68 when *Little House on the Prairie* was published. And she was still writing at age 76, when *These Happy Golden Years* was published.

Don't give up on your dreams. Reaching for your dreams will keep you young. And don't keep putting them off until tomorrow or you might end up like the lady who was stranded in her house during a flood. As the waters started to rise, a neighbor in an automobile drove by her house and told her to get in. She said, "No, that's okay, I'll wait." Later as the waters continued to rise still further, someone in a boat yelled at her to jump in. Still, she said, "No, that's okay, I'll wait." Finally, hours later (when the woman was on her roof), a helicopter pilot flew over her house and threw her a rope. But she declined a ride once again saying, "No, that's okay, I'll wait."

Soon after when the lady drowned and went to Heaven, she asked God, "Why did you let me drown down there?"

To which He replied, "I sent you a car, a boat, and a helicopter. I gave you every opportunity. You just wouldn't take it."

Don't wait for just the right time and miss your chance. If you want to write a book, start writing. If you want to learn to sing, start singing. If you want to learn Russian, УЗНАТЬ ЕГО. If you want to run a marathon, start running. If you want to climb Mt. Everest, start climbing. If you want to be an ornithologist, then get out those binoculars and start scanning tree branches for that elusive bird.

Your life is a work in progress; make your own unique path. Create your own special, one-of-a-kind life.

YOU MIGHT BE A DREAMER IF:
- ❖ You think mountains are for climbing.
- ❖ You think you can publish your first book when you're 65.

- ❖ You think you can start a successful second career at 50.
- ❖ You think you can start a successful third career at 70.
- ❖ You think there is still time for you to be President.
- ❖ You just don't know when to give up.

Chapter 9
GIRLS JUST WANNA HAVE FUN
Experience everything life has to offer - twice

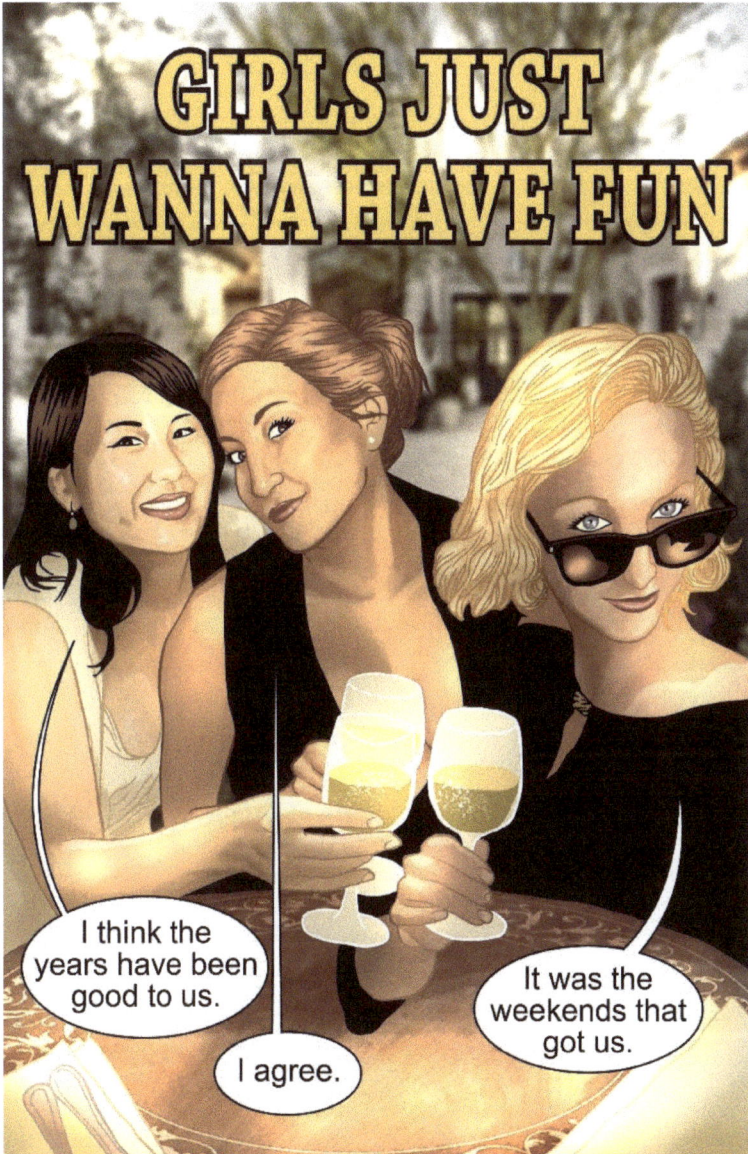

ATTRACTIVE WOMEN over the age of 50 are long overdue some respect. For decades, probably even centuries, the world has set forth a double standard. They say men get more "distinguished" as they age, while women just get "older."

What is that about and who came up with that distinction? Why the double standard? Well, you have to recall that women used to be considered the "property" of their husbands. They had to get their father's or their husband's approval to do practically anything. It wasn't until 1869, less than 150 years ago, that women were allowed to vote, but ONLY in Wyoming Territory. Nationwide women were not allowed to vote until 1920. A hundred fifty years may seem like a long time, but sociologically speaking, it's not.

Men were in charge of everything: government, real estate, education and most of the wealth for a very long time and they were given a certain respect because of that. Often as they aged, their wealth increased, earning them even more respect. Women were not given that opportunity. So, it was not unusual for older, established men to take younger wives.

Women have come a very long way from those days: with their own lives and their own careers, and we don't have to ask anyone's permission anymore.

Today, older women can attain just as much success and wealth as any man. And there really is no reason why an older, successful woman and a younger man cannot get together. A man can date someone half his age and no one seems to notice. But let an older woman step out with a younger man and see what happens. It's just another double standard for women. This is indicative of an internalized societal misogyny. There really should be no difference between an older man/younger woman relationship, and an older woman/younger man relationship. Personally, I prefer someone closer to my own age who likes to listen to the same music, watch the same movies, or just understands my jokes, because we are from the same generation. But it shouldn't be any different for a woman than it is for a man.

There are so many beautiful and successful women in America today over the age of 50. They should get the adoration they deserve, whether it's from a younger or an older man, or from society in general. And besides deserving adoration, women over 50 also deserve to have more fun.

And why don't we have more fun? Why are women always the responsible ones, while "the guys" get to go out and have fun? Why does a guy need a "man cave" to store all his toys? Why isn't there a girl's cave? Apparently, however, times are changing. I just saw a TV commercial where there was a reference to a "she shed". But why do most of us still work a full-time job, then come home, cook and clean and take care of the kids? Once a woman becomes pregnant, her life changes forever. It's not the same for men. For women, the partying and staying out late comes to a screeching halt, but a man can still go out with the guys every night and have a grand old time if he's so inclined.

Although motherhood is a precious thing and something most women desire, it might be even more wonderful for us after we've sown a few wild oats ourselves. Don't be in such a hurry to get married and begin having children. Enjoy your freedom while you can; motherhood takes a lot of time and attention.

Women can now have children without much risk until the age of 50. I'm not suggesting waiting until then to settle down and start a family, but get out and enjoy your life, your career and your relationship in your twenties, thirties, and forties. Indulge and nourish your creative side and your OWN inner child. Meet and date lots of guys, meet all kinds of people; meet so many people you can never remember all their names, experience other cultures, travel the world.

Can't afford it? Be a travel writer. Become a flight attendant. There's so much out there to experience, don't sell yourself short. Don't hit 60 and wonder why you never did so many things. And don't stop having fun just because you're "older." Just because you are older (50 or 60 or 80), doesn't mean you can't still enjoy your life. Find a reason to have something to look forward to. Don't ever think you're too old to have fun. You're only as old as you perceive yourself to be. Keep going, keep dreaming, keep having fun!

YOU MIGHT BE HAVING TOO MUCH FUN IF:

- ❖ All your neighbors have 9-1-1 on speed dial.
- ❖ You've already run out of pages to stamp on your passport (and it's only February).
- ❖ All the clerks at Party City know you by name.
- ❖ You refuse to date anyone older than 30 (and you're 73).
- ❖ Your bedtime is everyone else's wake-up time.

Chapter 10
GOLD DIGGER
Be your own Gold Digger

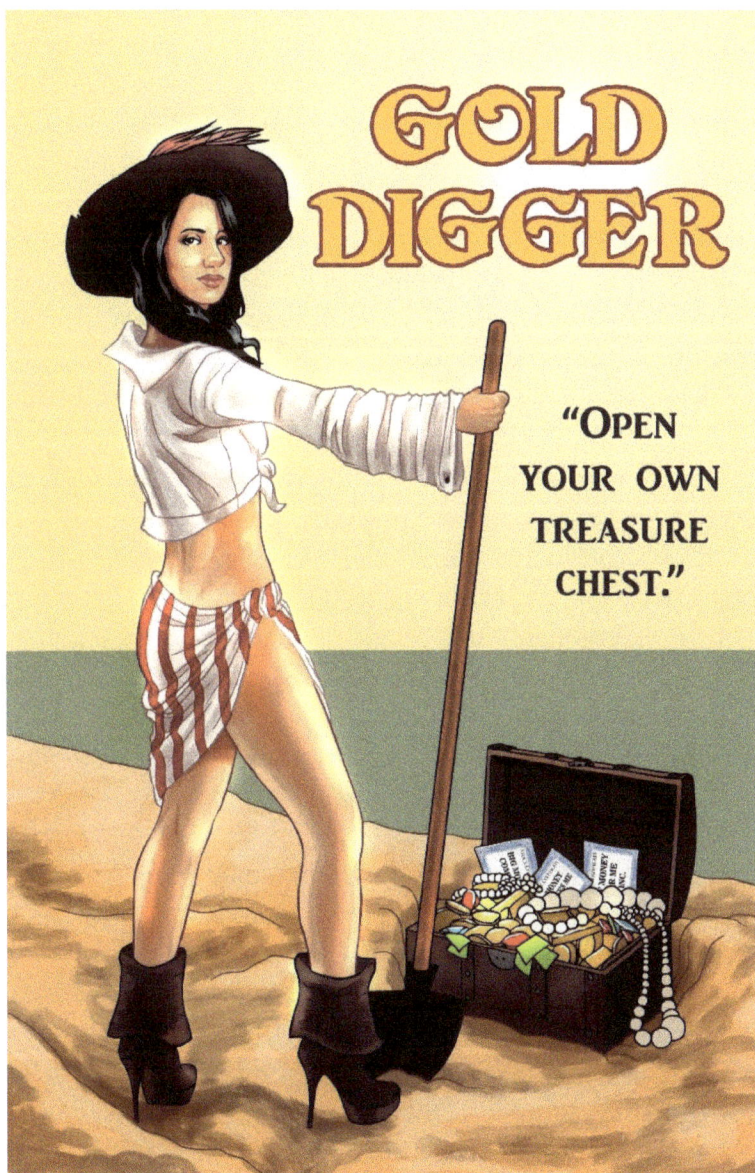

I KNOW WE'VE ALL HEARD the term "gold digger" (made famous in this generation by Kanye West) before. Someone is usually talking about a younger woman being with an older, more successful man, presumably for his money. "Look at that twenty-something with that 60-year-old guy; I'm sure she's with him for his fun personality. And he's with her for her intelligence." Yeah, right.

We've all heard it, thought it, or maybe even said it. In this day and age, it's possible the roles could be reversed, a younger attractive guy with a wealthy older woman. But usually it's the former: old rich guy with young attractive woman. Even in 2019, you still see this type of arrangement.

BLACK WIDOW

In the movie *Black Widow*, Teresa Russell gives new meaning to the term "gold digger."

Her "career path" includes doing extensive research on wealthy, older men and becoming their perfect woman. Whether as a blonde, brunette or redhead, she walks down the aisle several times. However, the marriages never seem to last very long. After a few short months, each new husband "mysteriously" dies in his sleep (while she is conveniently out of town) leaving his considerable fortune to his grief-stricken bride. In the end, Debra Winger, a determined FBI agent, puts an end to Russell's marrying and killing spree career.

Most of us, however, would probably prefer a less drastic means of finding success.

So, I'm here to suggest that we women be our own "gold diggers." Yes, go out and dig for our own gold, and thereby, our own power. Women are just as capable (if not more so) as men of making and investing money. In fact, women are often better investors. Women are more conservative, level-headed, and steady with their investments. Men tend to be more reckless and willing to take chances to make the big money on riskier investments. Like betting on a small biotech speculative stock to soar in value, which ends up plummeting instead. Women are more likely to be interested in premium quality stocks, which weather the ups and downs of time and of the stock market and do well in the long run.

But maybe you're saying, "That's all fine and good, but I don't have any money to begin to invest." Or maybe you're even in debt and don't see a way out. How do you get to that point where you can see a brighter financial future? Just take a deep breath and begin right where you are now. It may take a while, (after all, you didn't get into debt overnight) but you will feel so much better when that burden is off you.

There are several different suggestions about the best way to get out of debt. Some suggest paying off the credit cards with the highest interest rates first. Others say start with the credit card with the smallest balance and pay it off first. However, if you are eager to raise your credit score quickly, the best way is to pay on all the credit cards at once. As your balance on each card declines, your score will begin to improve. Once you have paid off two-thirds of your balances (on each card) and are only using one-third of your available credit, your credit score will go up dramatically.

Then select the card with the lowest balance and just concentrate on it exclusively. For now, quit using this card. Anytime you have an extra $20, make an extra payment on that card. You'll be surprised how quickly all those small payments will add up and your balance will be paid in full.

Then find a way to use your innate talent and intelligence and take advantage of our capitalistic society. If possible, start by going to college and getting a degree. If you can, it's best to stay in-state as it will make your tuition more reasonable and your student loans less burdensome.

But in the long run, a college degree will be worth it. The average dollar amount of lifetime earnings is around half a million dollars more for a college graduate than for a high school graduate. Unless you've got your own trust fund to fall back on, that's a lot of money. Women today are getting more education and earning more degrees than men. Women are more likely than men to enter college and less likely to drop out.

Today, the percentage of women graduating from college has exceeded the percentage of male graduates. In fact, women have earned almost 10 million more college degrees than men since 1982. In an article from AEI.org (American Enterprise Institute) by Mark Perry on May 13, 2013,[19] the following statistics were quoted:

> "According to data from the Department of Education on college degrees by gender, the US college degree gap favoring women started back in 1978, when for the first time ever, more women than men earned an Associate's degree. Five years later in 1982, women earned more Bachelor degrees than men for the first time, and women have increased their share of Bachelor's degrees in every year since then. In another five years by 1987, women earned the majority of Master's degrees for the first time. Finally, within another decade, more women than men earned doctor's degrees by 2006, and female domination of college degrees at every level was complete."

---

[19] http://www.aei.org/publication/stunning-college-degree-gap-women-have-earned-almost-10-million-more-college-degrees-than-men-since-1982/

In 2013, the percentages of women earning degrees were as follows: Associate degrees, 61.6 percent; Bachelor degrees, 56.7 percent; Master degrees, 59.9 percent; Doctorate degrees, 51.6 percent.

Men, however, do still outnumber women in law schools, medical and dental schools, but women are quickly closing the gap. Right now, they're close to 50/50, with men at approximately 53 percent and women at 47 percent. And the gap continues to close as more and more women enter these fields.

Areas in which women are still far behind their male counterparts are science, technology, engineering, and math. In 2010, only 12 percent of engineers were women. There are many theories about why there are so few women in these fields.

One interesting theory set forth by a young former Google employee, James Damore, is that it's simply a biological difference. In an interview on *Fox Business Channel* with Jim Varney on August 17th, 2017,[20] Damore said that these innate differences cause men to focus on things while women focus more on people. What causes this fundamental difference? According to Damore, prenatal testosterone is the culprit. Needless to say, his theory was not too well received in Silicon Valley. I did mention he's a *former* Google employee, didn't I?

However, in three areas of studies that require advanced degrees, women already outnumber men: optometry, pharmacy, and veterinary medicine.

So, if you want to have a lot of money to invest, go to college and stay as long as you can. If college is out of the question, find some kind of vocational training program. Unlike archaic vocational courses, which included mostly woodworking and auto-maintenance, today there are a

[20] https://video.foxbusiness.com/v/5543869822001/?#sp=show-clips

myriad of interests to choose from that can lead to good-paying jobs. Some of these programs require a two-year community college degree. Other programs can be completed in less than a year. Either way, these training programs can make a drastic difference in your earning potential. Here are just a few examples:

- Physical Therapist Assistant
- Pharmacy Technician
- Paralegal
- Court Reporter
- Physician's Assistant
- Health Physics Technician
- X-Ray Technician
- Radiation Therapist
- Ultrasound Sonographer
- Legal Secretary/Assistant
- Dental Hygienist
- Computer Security Analyst

I personally know women in all of these fields who do not have a college degree but make a very good living and can take care of themselves.

Other high-paying jobs that require little advanced training or training on the job:

- Real Estate Broker
- Financial Services Sales Agent
- Postal Service Workers
- Executive Administrative Assistant
- Elevator Installation/Repair
- Gaming Manager
- Railroad Operators/Repair
- Property Management
- Police Officers

- Detectives/Criminal Investigators
- Insurance Appraisers
- Claims Adjustors
- Welder
- Nuclear Monitor Technician & Operators
- Hotel Executive Chef
- Plumber
- Make-up Artist

Prefer to just sit at a desk and make good money without going to college?

If you have technical skills, it should be easy.

According to Laurence Bradford, here are *13 High Paying Tech Careers You Can Get Without a College Degree:*[21]

- Computer User Support Specialist
- Junior Data Analyst
- Computer Network Support Specialist
- Digital Marketer
- Cyber Security Analyst
- Multimedia Artist
- Web Developer
- Web Designer/Front End Developer
- Aerospace Engineering & Operations Technician
- Mobile App Developer
- Software Engineer
- Information Technology Manager
- DevOps Engineer

Another area in which women have made great strides recently is in politics. There is now a record number of women in Washington after the last 2018 election – 95

---

[21] https://www.forbes.com/sites/laurencebradford/2016/07/06/13-high-paying-tech-careers-you-can-get-without-a-college-degree/#6f142b691223

women in the House of Representatives; 33 women in the Senate; and six women governors. Included in this new group of representatives are the first Native American woman, the first Muslim woman, the first Latina woman, the first women of color from the states of Connecticut and Massachusetts, the youngest women in the House of Representatives, and the first US women senators from the states of Arizona and Tennessee.

So, get out and start shaking hands and telling everyone what your opinion is on everything. By the way, the pay is very good for politicians at the national level – well over $100,000 a year. And apparently YOU get paid even when the government is shut down (unlike your local mail person).

So, find something that interests you and get an education or training. Then start mining and digging for your OWN gold.

It's 2019; we don't need a man to provide for us. We can provide for ourselves. We can dig for our own gold.

YOU MIGHT BE A GOLD DIGGER IF:
- ❖ You ask someone their credit score before you know their name.
- ❖ You only date men who carry an AARP card AND a Black American Express.
- ❖ You call ALL your dates "POPS."
- ❖ You only accept fine jewelry, deeds of trust or gold bars on Valentine's Day.
- ❖ You're always the only one in the room born after World War II.

Chapter 11
DIAMONDS ARE A GIRL'S BEST FRIEND
Just Make Sure They're Investment Grade.

IF YOU ARE going to live to be ageless, you'll need financial security. You need to learn how to invest all the money you're going to make or have made in your lifetime. Remember, as a college graduate or as a graduate from a specialized vocational program, you are going to earn a lot of money and you will want to invest it wisely.

Start out by paying yourself first. Take a portion of each paycheck, at least 15 percent, and open a savings account. Another option is to have your employer take that amount and invest in a company savings plan. Many companies will match part of your contributions. Take control of your own finances. Don't think that someone else, like a father, a husband or even a broker is a better investor than you are; they're not. And no one cares more about your money than you do.

As we discussed earlier, women are more savvy investors. According to Fidelity Investments, women outperform men in their investments.[22] Men tend to be more confident and take risks, while women take a more stable, long-term approach.

According to Sallie Krawcheck, who has had a successful career on Wall Street, it is important for women to become financially savvy.[23]

---

[22] https://www.fidelity.com/about-fidelity/individual-investing/better-investor-men-or-women

[23] https://money.cnn.com/2017/03/08/investing/women-better-investors-than-men/index.html

Krawcheck, who has started a financial firm specifically for women called Ellevest, says, "Invest like a woman, because money is power."

In a CNN interview with Maggie Lakes, Krawcheck said, "We women will not be fully equal with men until we are financially equal with men." She declared 2017 as the "Year of Financial Feminism."

It's important to learn about the stock market. Anyone can open a stock trading account. And you can purchase your stocks online without a broker's assistance. A good place to start investing is by looking for established companies that pay dividends.

In fact, there is a group of companies called "Dividend Aristocrats" that have steadily and reliably paid dividends to their shareowners for the past 50 years. Not surprisingly, these stocks have a much higher rate of return than non-dividend paying stocks.

Consider adding bonds to your investment portfolio. Also, if used conservatively, options can be a great way to increase your investments. But please, be very conservative with options. One way to use options to your benefit is to sell options (not buy) on stocks you already own. You get paid extra cash for stocks you already own by giving someone else the "option" of buying the stock from you at a certain price.

And don't be afraid to consider investing in the real estate market by buying not only your own home or condo, but also investing in rental property. Invest in condos or houses that can easily be rented out to the average family or perhaps college students. This type of investment can provide additional monthly income and long-term appreciation. However, investing in real estate is more involved than investing in the stock market.

If you want your money out of the stock market, it takes only seconds. Real estate investments must be managed and maintained and can take months to sell. Not everyone has the expertise and the patience for investing in real estate. Also, unexpected repairs and frequent vacancies can make real estate investing challenging. However, for those who can do it, it can be very profitable. I have a friend who buys rental property, does all the renovation work herself, and then manages the property herself.

So, women can make their own money and invest it wisely.

But don't women spend a lot more money than men?

Not really. Women may spend on household and living expenditures, but men often buy expensive big-ticket items like boats, golf clubs, and motorcycles when they go shopping. And according to the same Fidelity Investments study as previously mentioned, women save more money than men.

So why do women often still marry for money and security instead of for love or passion? Studies show that women are still very interested in a man's credit score. Even though we may have a successful career or a good job, women still often look for a man to take care of them.

It's fine to desire a reliable, responsible mate and potential father, but the days of needing a man to take care of us financially are over. If you need someone financially, they will always have that power over you.

Give yourself the freedom to find someone for love, not money. Don't think just because someone is successful that he would make a good mate. In my younger years I was tempted to marry someone who was a lawyer, a CPA and very wealthy. He had all the right credentials (on paper). There was only one problem. He just didn't make me happy. I am so glad I moved on. I know my life has been much more rewarding and happier by finding that "right" someone who does make me happy.

Don't ever give your freedom and happiness away for any man, no matter how much money or power he has. Trust me, it's just not worth it. And in the long run, you will pay dearly.

So it's best to make and invest your own money.

UNUSUAL INVESTMENTS

What are some other kinds of investments besides stocks, bonds, and real estate?

There are a number of other less practical and unusual ways that people invest their money. You only have to watch a few episodes of *Strange Inheritance* or *Pawn Stars* to get an idea of where people put their money.

Some people invest millions of dollars in art or diamonds or first edition books. Many buy classic cars, yachts, or rare coins. Some invest in comic books, antique dolls, toy soldiers, sailing ships and stamps.

Many of these kinds of "investments" are really more of a hobby than an investment.

Of course, different people enjoy collecting vastly different things. One guy invested millions of dollars creating elaborate opera dolls and a miniature opera set and putting on opera performances for audiences.

Many of these objects are valuable and do go up in value (the definition of a good investment), but their values can vary greatly from year to year. Many of these items can be difficult and time consuming to sell, and an investment is only as good as someone is willing to pay for it at any given time.

So that diamond may be pretty and sparkly, but just be sure it's "investment grade" so that when you go to sell it, you get what it's worth.

YOU MIGHT BE OBSESSED WITH INVESTING IF:

- ❖ You turn on *Squawk Box* before you turn on your coffeemaker.
- ❖ You jam up the checkout line at Walmart because you're complaining to the clerk about their Second Quarter earnings.
- ❖ You buy a bottle of Dom Perignon every time the Dow hits a new high.
- ❖ You order a prospectus in the drive-thru lane at McDonalds instead of a Big Mac.
- ❖ You spend more time with *Mad Money*'s Jim Cramer than you do with your husband.

Chapter 12
WHAT'S IN A NAME?
"A Rose by any other name…"

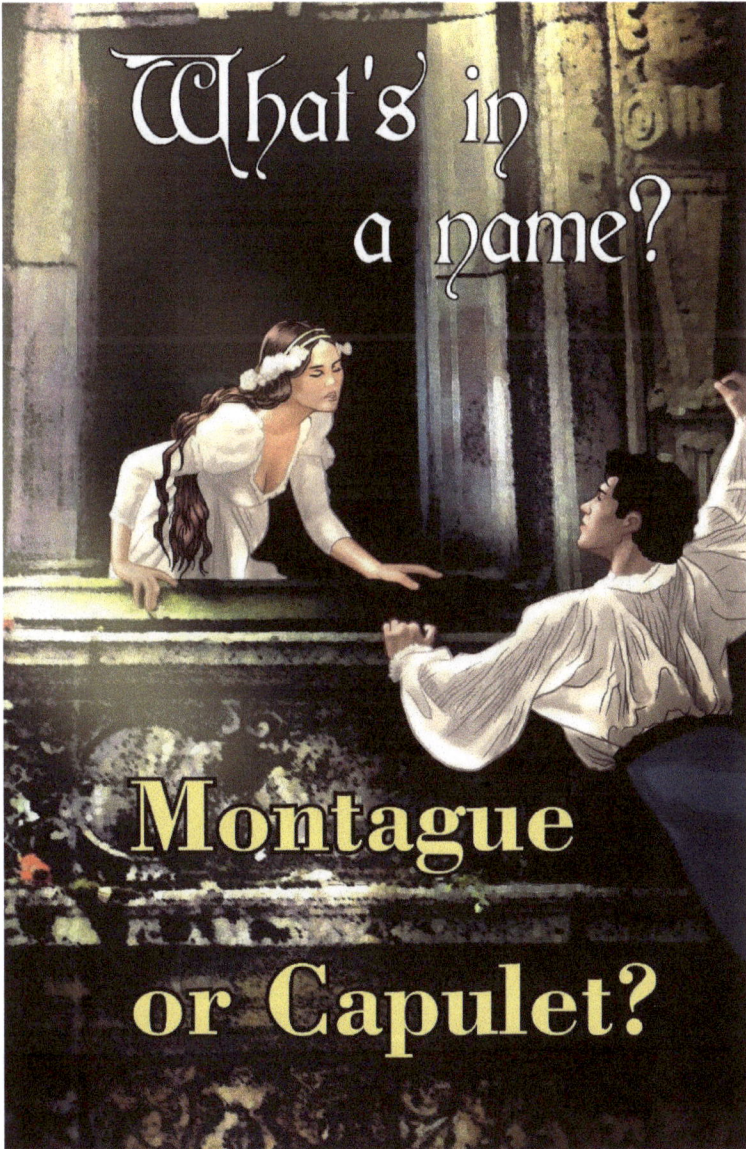

What's in a name?

Montague or Capulet?

AS AGELESS WOMEN, we have a lot to offer to our families, our communities, our careers, and our society in general. We are strong women with confidence in ourselves and our abilities. We don't need a man to take care of us, to provide for us, to "own" us. We are strong and independent. We have created a life for ourselves. We know who we are. We have made a name for ourselves.

Then why, I wonder, are we so willing to give our name up so easily? As soon as the "right" guy pops that magic four-word question and we answer in the affirmative, we become someone else. We are no longer Jane Doe, the person we have spent a lifetime becoming. We are suddenly Mrs. John Smith. What is that supposed to mean, anyhow?

Have we become the female (Mrs.) version of John Smith? Or perhaps we have become the property of John Smith and must wear his brand, so everyone will know we are now taken.

Either way doesn't sound like too appealing of an option.

John Smith is still John Smith the day after the wedding, but Jane Doe has literally given up her name and who she is (or was). She has become a different person in every sense of the word, certainly legally. Her identity, as it was, has been erased.

Have you ever tried to find an old girlfriend from high school or college who has changed her name? It's not easy.

But you might say, "It's just a name. I'm still the same person I always was."

If that's the case, then why do we change our names in the first place? Why can't we just stay who we are like our husband does? Why exactly do we change our names when we get married? How did this custom begin? And an even better question: why are we still following it?

Let's look at where this tradition came from and why we continue to adhere to it.

The concept of a woman taking her husband's name has been around a long time. As women were considered the property of their husbands, it was only natural for them to take their husband's last name.

In an article on *The Flor-Ala* by Jasmine Fleming[24] sociology professor Amber Paulk says that women taking their husband's name has a deep historical and cultural background:

> "When you look back at the history of marriage as an institution, women were considered property. They were moving from a father's home to a husband's home. It would make total sense for them to take their husband's name.
>
> Most cultures were founded with a patriarchal structure where men dominated the economics. It's fairly recent that women have been able to change positions in society. Women have only been allowed to vote in the United States for less than one hundred years."

However, the idea of keeping one's maiden name has been floating around for quite some time in the minds of some women. A women's rights activist and feminist named Lucy Stone supported women keeping their name as far back as the 1850s. However, the idea has taken a long time to catch on. But as the Feminist movement became popular in the 1970s, so did the idea of maintaining one's identity by keeping one's maiden name.

---

[24]   https://www.florala.net/life/name-change-in-marriage-cultural-tradition/article_e142fb1c-1b0a-11e3-98d8-0019bb30f31a.html

Since then, the number of women who have decided to keep their own last name has risen each decade. According to an article in *The New York Times* by Claire Cain Miller and Derek Willis,[25] in the 1980s, only 14 percent kept their names. In 1990, that number had risen to 16.2 percent. But by the year 2000, it had grown to 26 percent. In 2014, 29.5 percent of women chose to keep their maiden name.

Of course, that means that more than two-thirds of women still chose to follow tradition and take their husband's names. According to an article by Daniel Luzer in *Salon*,[26] apparently younger women are much more likely to keep their names. Sixty-three percent of women who married in their twenties took their husband's names. Eighty percent of women who married in their thirties took their husband's name. And 91 percent of women in their sixties chose to take their husband's name.

Obviously, the older generations would be more accepting of traditional norms and probably less questioning of other alternatives, such as keeping their own names. Yet there is a certain group of more mature women who ARE more likely to keep their maiden names. These are women who are already accomplished in their lives and careers and are unwilling to give up that name recognition.

For example, a well-known actress or singer, a medical doctor with an established practice, a lawyer who is a partner in a law firm with her name on the door, or a writer with her name on a bestseller.

All of these women, at any age, would be more likely to keep their maiden names.

So, what options DO women have when deciding what their name will be after they walk down the aisle?

---

[25]   https://www.nytimes.com/2015/06/28/upshot/maiden-names-on-the-rise-again.html

[26]https://www.salon.com/2013/07/14/study_married_women_who_keep_their_maiden_names_more_successful_than_those_who_dont_partner/

According to an article by Angie Siu on *Mic*,[27] here are some of the options:

- Keep her own name
- Take his and make hers a middle name (Hillary Rodham Clinton)
- Take his legally but use her professionally
- Hyphenate (Farrah Fawcett-Majors)

Of course, yet still another option, is to make up an entirely new name for the bride and groom.

It can be a difficult decision to choose which way to go with so many options. But it's just something all women everywhere have to deal with, right?

Well, not really. I was surprised to learn that the United States is somewhat unique in its practice of women taking their husband's name upon marriage. There are many places in the world where a woman is simply *not allowed by law* to take her husband's surname.

According to an article in *TIME* by Jacob Koffler,[28] here are some of the places where women are not only expected to keep their maiden names, but legally *cannot* change their names:

- In Quebec, women are forbidden from taking their husband's name after marriage. The Quebec Charter of Rights, which promotes gender equality to names, went into effect in 1976.
- In Greece there is also a law, which went into effect in 1983, which requires all women to keep their maiden name.

---

[27]https://mic.com/articles/55317/more-women-are-keeping-their-own-names-after-marriage-says-facebook#.ot6inSNMg
[28] http://time.com/3940094/maiden-married-names-countries/

- In France there is a law going back all the way to 1789 that says no one can use a name other than the one on their birth certificate. Women cannot legally change their name after marriage.
- In Italy women cannot legally change their name. This has been the case since 1975. Italian women, however, are given the option of adding their husband's last name on to theirs.
- In Belgium a person cannot change their last name after marriage.
- In the Netherlands, a woman is only recognized by her maiden name.
- In Malaysia and Korea women keep their maiden names.
- Also, in most Spanish speaking countries, including Spain and Chile, women retain their birth names.

So, it would seem that the idea that a woman should take her husband's last name is not a universally accepted one.

I found it very interesting that even in Middle Eastern countries, such as Iran, Yemen, Jordan and Syria, the Muslim women maintain their maiden names out of respect to their fathers.

In the name game, yet another possibility is for the husband to take the bride's last name.

If you've ever watched the comedy series *Newhart*, you'll remember the episode where all Michael (Peter Scolari) has to do for Stephanie's (Julia Duffy) rich parents to buy them a mansion on the hill is to take Stephanie's last name (Vanderkellen). Michael desperately wants to move into the mansion but is struggling with the idea of giving up his name. When Michael asks Bob Newhart's advice, Newhart says, "A man's name is all he has. You can't just give your name away." Then Newhart's wife, Joanna (Mary

Frann), says, "Well, I did when I married you." To which Dick replies, "That's different, you're a woman."

In the long run, Michael was unable to relinquish his name and they moved into Newhart's carriage house instead of the mansion.

But men taking their bride's last name is becoming more common according to *yourtango.com* (author Mary Schwager)[29]. Jake Wolff of Hitchswitch, a name changing service, has helped more than 2000 couples change their names. Five percent of the name changes were men. Three percent took their wife's last name and 2 percent arranged a hybrid or hyphenated name.

Wolff says the trend is increasing.

Many a couple has struggled with merging their love and their names into one.

The most important thing to remember is that it is your choice. No one can tell you that you have to take someone else's name or that you should keep your maiden name. The decision is yours and your spouse's. No one can tell you what to do. What works best for you and your spouse is the right decision.

Can you imagine how difficult it would be to select a last name if you had to choose between Montague or Capulet? Perhaps the story of Romeo and Juliet would have turned out differently if Juliet had just decided to become Juliet Capulet Montague, thereby appeasing both families.

For a happier ending, you might want to emulate Elizabeth Barrett Browning and Robert Browning instead.

Hopefully, whatever you decide to call yourself can be resolved without bloodshed and you can live happily ever after.

---

[29]   http://www.yourtango.com/experts/galtime-com/more-men-taking-their-wives-last-name

YOU MIGHT HAVE CHOSEN THE WRONG LAST NAME IF:

- ❖ Your wedding announcement needs an addendum.
- ❖ Your last name is now Rothensteinberg, McGillacutty & Ali.
- ❖ People's eyes glaze over by the time you're through introducing yourself.
- ❖ People burst out in laughter every time you introduce yourself.
- ❖ People think you're telling them the name of the law firm where you work instead of YOUR name.
- ❖ Your last name is Butt and your husband's name is Head.

Chapter 13
MIND OVER MATTER
Where the Mind Goes, the Body Will Follow

WE'VE ALL HEARD this saying before. Most often it's used referring to aging. If we don't mind, we're yet another year older, then it doesn't really matter.

Someone could use the phrase, "you're only as young as you feel," or "you're only as old as you think you are." If this were true, we could all just think we're only 30 and get on with our lives. We'd never have to think about those nasty telltale numbers on top of our birthday cake again.

While it may not be quite that easy, there could be something to this familiar sentiment of staying young simply by believing it. We've all seen and known people in their forties who look and act like they're 104. People who seem to be miserable physically, mentally, and emotionally no matter what their life is like. Then there are those people who are 104 who act like they're in their forties- smiling, happy, surrounded by friends and family, looking forward to putting yet another candle on top of that birthday cake of life.

How can this be? Can one's attitude about themselves and what's happening around them make that drastic of a difference? How powerful is the power of the mind over the body?

I'm reminded of a story about identical twin boys. One day they were tested to see how they would react to the exact circumstances in a controlled setting. Each boy was put into a room that had been filled with all kinds of toys and music and games. Then a small pile of manure was also placed in each room. They were left in the room alone for one hour.

When they opened the door, the first boy was sitting quietly in the corner and hadn't touched any of the toys. When they asked why he didn't play with the toys, his reply was he was afraid to go near the manure to get to the toys.

When they opened the second door, the other twin was running, jumping, and playing with every toy in the room and was completely covered in manure. When they asked him, "Why did you get so close to that stinky pile?" his response was, "Well, with that much manure, I figured there had to be a pony in there somewhere."

And yes, we've all been in that room at some point in our lives. How we interpret and respond to our surroundings can make all the difference.

Remember the movie *Cocoon* where Don Ameche and other senior citizens discover their very own "fountain of youth" in an abandoned swimming pool? All the elderly people began to experience renewed strength and vitality after taking a dip in the pool. Later in the film we find out that the elixir they have discovered is otherworldly and aliens have been using the pool for breeding, giving the water its rejuvenating properties.

While the senior citizens eventually lost their literal fountain of youth, they developed a whole different perspective and mindset toward aging. They discovered that maybe the fountain of youth isn't literally a fountain or even a swimming pool at all.

Maybe the fountain of youth is a lot closer than we think. What if it's inside each and every one of us – in our minds? What if we could constantly and consistently convince our mind that we were not really aging? Not just mentally, but physically.

It's a nice sentiment, but it couldn't be true. Or could it? According to psychologist Ellen Langer it can be true, and she proved it.

And it has nothing to do with aliens.

In a 1981 experiment now called "the counter-clockwise study," Langer told participants – all men in their seventies and eighties – that by the end of the process they would be feeling like it was 1959 again (20 years earlier).

Not only were her expectations high for this study, but the participants also were made to feel a high degree of expectation.

The experiment was divided into two groups of men. Both groups were men in the same age range and physical conditions. Both groups were put in the same environment. The only difference was that one group was told to reminisce about their younger days. This was the control group; the other group was told to act AS IF they really were living in their younger days.

Before the experiment all the men were given evaluations of their mental and physical conditions. Several factors such as flexibility, hearing, vision, memory and even intelligence were all tested.

Then the experiment began.

While it was impossible to literally return the men to 1959, Langer decided to bring 1959 to them. She created an environment in which everything was the same as it had been in their 20-year past and then put the men inside it and told them to act AS IF it really was 1959.

According to an article in *The New York Times Magazine* article by Bruce Grierson,[30] the experiment began when eight men in their seventies stepped out of a van in front of a converted monastery in New Hampshire. They shuffled forward, a few of them stooped from arthritis, a couple even with canes. Then they passed through the door and entered a time warp. Perry Como crooned on a vintage radio. Ed

---

[30] https://www.nytimes.com/2014/10/26/magazine/what-if-age-is-nothing-but-a-mind-set.html?_r=0

Sullivan welcomed guests on a black and white television set. Everything inside – including the books on the shelves and the magazines (*Life* & *The Saturday Evening Post*) lying around – were designed to conjure 1959.

There were no mirrors or recent photos to shatter the illusion of the past.

Each day the men listened to music popular in the 1950s and watched movies starring actors from the '50s. They discussed events from the '50s as if they really were current events. Topics such as the first United States satellite launch, Castro's victory in Cuba, and how fear was causing many people in the United States to feel the need for bomb shelters.

Of course, being men, the subject of sports was popular. They talked about sports figures such as Johnny Unitas, Wilt Chamberlain, and Mickey Mantle as if they were still winning championship games.

At week's end, all the men were tested again. The results were truly amazing!

Langer recorded that both the control group and the experimental group showed improvement in several areas including "physical strength, manual dexterity, gait, posture, perception, memory, cognition sensitivity, hearing and even vision."

The men seemed to sit and stand taller and have more confidence in themselves. Even their intelligence scores improved.

Of the men who lived like it was 1959, 63 percent showed higher IQ scores while the percentage improvement for the control group was only in the forties.

Langer, who has been called the "the mother of positive psychology," says, "They put their minds in an earlier time, and their bodies went along for the ride."

The men, who had taken before and after photos, were judged to actually be younger in the "after" photos by individuals who were not part of the experiment.

The icing on the cake of the study was when the participants, many who had seemed physically and mentally lackadaisical at best at the first of the week, burst into a touch football game while waiting for their bus ride home.

By changing their physical environment and surroundings and controlling what they were exposed to, AND changing their mindset, these men actually "became" younger.

Then in 2010, the BBC broadcasted a similar experiment called *The Young Ones*.

According to Grierson, six aging former celebrities were the guinea pigs this time.

The stars were driven in classic cars to a country home designed inside and out to look and feel like it was 1975. The inhabitants were immersed in that era because everything in the house was from the 1970s.

After a week of living in the year 1975, they came out renewed physically and mentally, and actually showed improved test scores on aging criteria, just as the men in the counterclockwise study had.

For example, one participant who had needed assistance in dressing himself at the beginning of the week, was gliding around gracefully hosting a party by the end of the week.

Even more dramatic, one of the celebrities who had arrived in a wheelchair left it behind and walked out with a cane instead.

Most of the other participants in the study seemed younger and even taller. They were made to feel relevant and important again and it showed in their bodies.

Langer also conducted a study in a hair salon in 2009 to examine the relationship between expectations of aging and physiological signs of health. This study was made up completely of women.

Forty-seven women between the ages of 27 and 83 were at a hair salon to have their hair cut, styled and/or colored. Before their hair appointment began, the women filled out a questionnaire and had their blood pressure taken. After their hair was done, they filled out a questionnaire about how they felt they looked. Then their blood pressure was taken again.

According to Langer, those women who saw themselves as looking younger after their makeover experienced a drop in blood pressure.

According to Grierson, Langer was also involved in another study involving all women. Eighty-four chambermaids were asked if they got much exercise, to which most replied "No."

The women were then encouraged to look at their work as exercise. When they did this, they realized they were getting a lot of exercise.

Once their mindset was changed, the women began to lose weight, even though they were not changing anything else. The women lost weight, showed an improved body mass index, and enhanced hip to waist ratio.

Once again showing that wherever you put your mind, your body will follow.

Langer is now doing research with avatars. In one particularly promising scenario, an individual can watch themselves playing tennis. The idea is that the mind will become involved as if it is moving and playing and the body will respond to this stimulus in kind. The jury is still out as to whether we can drop a few pounds this way or not.

By the way, this probably won't be the last you hear of Ellen Langer and the counterclockwise experiment. Just as the story of *Cocoon* ended up in Hollywood, Langer's story is likely to end up on the big screen. The word is that Jennifer Aniston will play the younger version of Langer in the movie.

What if we could all recreate these kinds of experiments and make ourselves younger? What if we could all create our own "fountain of youth" right inside our own mind? What would it take?

Would we have to convince ourselves that it's 1959 and we're dancing with Fred Astaire? Or that it's 1979 and we're "doing the hustle" wearing bell bottoms and platform shoes? Or that we're on the tennis court lobbying balls with Serena or Venus Williams or both?

Well, maybe, and why not? Swing that imaginary tennis racket or make a few extra beds and call it exercise. Get your heart rate up and drop those pounds. Get out those dancing shoes and that '70s disco ball.

Apparently, being immersed in music, movies and events from a previous time not only makes us feel better, but actually takes us back (on some level) to that time. We FEEL in our minds like we're really there and our body follows suit. If we can change and control our environment and control how our mind responds to it, we just might have the biggest secret yet to reverse aging. Our minds think it's 20 years ago, and so our bodies go along.

If it makes me feel, look and act 20 or 30 or even 3 years younger, I'm willing to give it a try.

What about you?

YOU MIGHT BE GETTING OLDER IF:

❖ It takes you AND three of your friends to blow out all your birthday candles.

❖ You're not sure why the Fire Department keeps showing up at your birthday parties.

❖ You buy Blue Emu by the case instead of the jar.

❖ Every story you tell starts with: "Well, back in 19_ _."

❖ The Express Checkout Lane at the grocery store is just too fast for you.

❖ When you talk about that crazy younger generation, you're referring to the Baby Boomers.

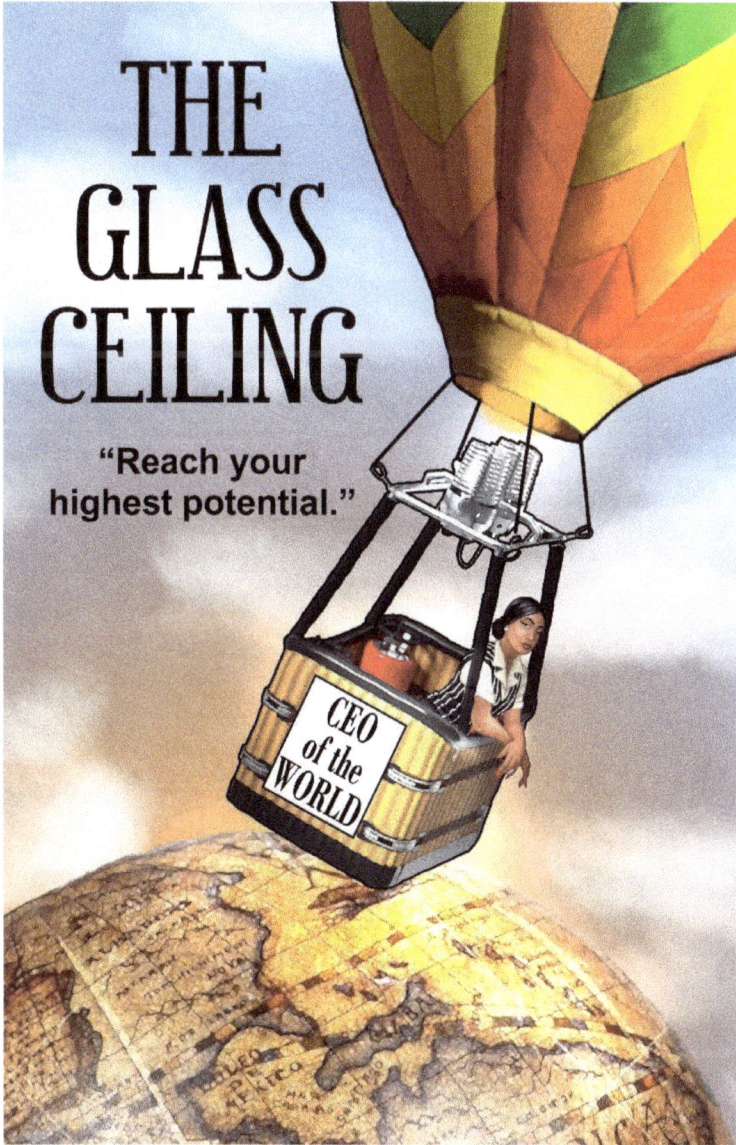

AS AGELESS WOMEN, many of us have careers that are very important to us. We get an education, and we work hard to get ahead in our chosen careers. For many of us, being able to get into the club and "break that glass ceiling" is an important part of our vocational journey. I know in my twenties and early thirties, it was my goal.

I wanted to get as far ahead in my company as I possibly could. I was willing to relocate to anywhere to get that next big or even small promotion. I wanted to climb that corporate ladder no matter where it took me as long as it was up.

And that's what it takes. You have to be willing to do whatever the company wants if you expect to get ahead. You must play their game. You must make the right connections and say the right things to the right people at the right time.

For many of you climbing that corporate ladder to that glass ceiling might be your chosen journey also. You might choose to try to go straight to the top through the traditional routes. For years, that is what I did, moving every few months to a better paying and more prestigious job. I was even fortunate enough to have several jobs I enjoyed and was able to do what I liked, which was public relations and writing.

And the pay, not to mention the benefits, was good because I worked for a large corporation. However, in general, the statistics on women breaking the glass ceiling are not promising.

In fact, if you really want to make it to the top of the corporate world, you might want to consider moving to another country.

According to a study done by the Grant Thornton International Business Report in 2014,[31] the United States lagged far behind in the number of women in top management positions.

In an article in *Business News Daily*, entitled "When it Comes to Women in Management, U.S. Doesn't Lead," Chad Brooks reported[32] that in the U.S., women account for only about 22 percent of senior managers.

In comparison, Russia ranked first in the ratings with a very respectable 43 percent of female managers. Other countries ranking high on the list were Indonesia, the Philippines, China, and Thailand. The United States just barely surpassed the United Kingdom, which reported 20 percent for female senior managers. The US did also fare better than Denmark, Germany, India, United Aram Emirates, Switzerland, and the Netherlands. Japan came in dead last with only 9 percent of women in senior management.

The Pew Research Center also states that men far outnumber women in senior management positions in the U.S.[33] Only 5 percent of chief executives in US companies in the Fortune 500 were women. In 2014, that meant that only 24 women were CEOs. However, this is progress. In 2010, only 2.4 percent of Fortune 500 companies' CEOs were female. And 20 years earlier there were none. Also, the larger the company, the less likely there will be a woman at the helm.

Little did I know I was about to hit my own glass ceiling, hard. Everything was great until I got yet another

---

[31] https://www.grantthornton.global/globalassets/1.-member-firms/global/insights/article-pdfs/2014/ibr2014_wib_report_final.pdf
[32] https://www.businessnewsdaily.com/6050-us-ranks-in-bottom-10-for-women-in-management-roles.html
[33] http://www.pewresearch.org/fact-tank/2014/08/07/perceptions-about-women-leaders-improve-but-gap-remains/

promotion. This time, even though I was another rung up the corporate ladder, I hated my job. I was in a position where every move I made was monitored. It was like living in a fishbowl.

Often women in higher management positions or in middle management trying to move higher can be highly visible and feel a lot of added pressure to represent not only themselves but all women.

Soon my dream job became a nightmare. The job itself was very stressful with constant deadlines. When I took the job I thought other people would be contributing, but I soon found out that "editor" meant I did all the interviews, wrote everything myself, took the photos, and did the layout. I did everything but deliver the magazine door to door.

I could work as late as I wanted to if I was early the next day. If I was 20 seconds late for work, my boss (actually my boss' boss) would let everyone in the building know about it. They couldn't help but hear him yelling. (And I don't think he liked my comment about his mouthwash, either). Apparently in his previous career he was an Army Colonel and still expected blind obedience and perhaps a different salute than the one I wanted to give him. I think he thought I was his own Private Benjamin who needed his tutelage. Or maybe he just wanted to make a man out of me. I, however, was not interested.

Even though I was getting rave reviews for my work, I began to dread having to show up at the office at all. My sleek, high-rise office building began to feel much more like a high security prison, and I was about to make my escape.

One day, I was driving down the road after having put the latest edition to bed when out of nowhere my heart began to race. I thought it was going to burst out of my chest. I had never had anything like that happen before. Of course, I thought I was having a heart attack.

I went to the emergency room to have it checked out. Although I was having some irregular heartbeats, what I really was experiencing was an anxiety attack – my first and my last. At that point, I decided I wasn't going back. I stayed for a couple more months, but mentally I had already checked out. When I left for Christmas vacation, I just never returned.

During this period, I had become very close friends with a lovely older gentleman who worked for the same company. We had our breaks at the same time, so we fell into an easy camaraderie discussing this and that, life, family, how much I hated my situation and what he was going to do when he retired. The day finally came when he retired, and he was so happy to start his new life in retirement. Even though I missed our conversations, I was happy for him.

One day I came into work (about three weeks after he retired) to the tragic news that he had passed away. I couldn't believe it; it seemed so unfair. He had worked for 30 years so he could retire and three weeks later he was gone!

After the disbelief and sadness subsided, I began to feel something else. All of a sudden, I knew I did not want to be there in 30 years. I did not want to put my life on hold for the next 30 years. I wanted to start living it right then. His untimely death gave me the extra impetus I needed to get out and start over.

I had made it to the top of my glass ceiling and realized I did not want to go any further. I fact, I didn't want to be on the corporate ladder at all anymore. So instead of reaching for the next rung, I took another step and jumped off the other side of the ladder.

Actually, things turned out pretty much the same for me as they did for Private Benjamin. I could relate to the scene where Goldie Hawn threw her bridal veil into the air and walked away from all the men (her dead husband, her father, her commanding officer, and her husband-to-be) in her life trying to tell her what to do. I especially liked the part where she punched her groom before she walked out. I, too, had had just about enough of other people (mostly men) trying to control my life, and decided to take responsibility for myself, my career, and my life.

After all the time, effort, relocations and saying the right things at the right time and getting along with the right people, I just wasn't interested anymore. It was like the perfect storm had happened in my professional life. I just wanted out. I no longer wanted to be in a corporate environment. I wanted to be free. So, I left. I took a few months off to decide what I wanted to do next.

What I wanted to do was travel. So, I went to work for an airline and was able to travel anywhere for free. Suddenly, I didn't mind being on time for work because I was following my dream. I wanted to be there. Even when I wasn't working, I could just "pop" on a plane with a bag thrown over my shoulder and go anywhere I wanted. Of course, this was before you had to do a striptease before you could board.

This was a very exciting and freeing time of my life. I "worked" and traveled for several months until I got the wanderlust out of my system, often traveling by myself to various cities. I'm glad I didn't wait to travel until I retired as so many people say they are going to do. You just never know what the future has in store.

After my job at the airline, I went back to graduate school, planning to finish my Ph.D. in Psychology. While in school, however, I went for a part-time job interview on a lark. The job was as a fashion representative for a women's clothing company. This temporary part-time job turned into a full-time permanent career for the next 10 years and I loved every minute of it. I was able to continue to travel and have my freedom. I even picked up more fashion lines and was a representative for several companies. Of course, I still had a "corporate" job, but every day was a different location with different people. It really did not even feel like work.

Once I left what wasn't right for me, I was able to live my life on my own terms. It was a little scary at first, but I am thankful I made my own choices instead of staying put because it was safer and easier. I would not be the same person I am today if I had stayed on my journey up the corporate ladder.

What would be different? All the things and places I would never have seen; the satisfaction of having a job that I loved; and all the hundreds of people I would never have met.

Not that there would have been anything wrong with my life if I had stayed. There were a lot of good people who are still there. And maybe I would have made in all the way to the top. But I have never regretted my decision. I know if I had stayed there, I would not have experienced life as fully as I have.

But if climbing that corporate ladder to the glass ceiling is your chosen journey, you might want to look at alternate paths to get you there. Maybe there is a side door, a back door, an open window or maybe you can just parachute through that glass ceiling. You could even bypass the glass ceiling all together by becoming your own boss and starting your own business. Or why not climb the corporate ladder while living in paradise?

If you want your corporate cake and a vacation spot to eat it too, you might consider checking out Jamaica. The *Jamaica Observer* says[34] that according to a study by the (ILO)

---

[34] http://www.jamaicaobserver.com/news/Jamaica-has-highest-percentage-of-women-managers-globally---ILO-report

International Labour Organization, Jamaica has the highest percentage of women managers globally.

The study entitled "Women in Business and Management, Gaining Momentum,"[35] found that the percentage of women managers in Jamaica was a whopping 59.3 percent.

Hey, man (and wo-man); don't worry; be happy.

Stay away from Yemen, though, if you want to be a CEO. Only a dismal 2.1 percent of women there ever make it into senior management.

It doesn't matter how you get there as long as it's your choice and your way.

YOU MIGHT HAVE HIT THE GLASS CEILING TOO HARD IF:

- ❖ You're still at work when your co-workers start to arrive the next morning.
- ❖ The last time you took a vacation the Cleveland Indians won the World Series.
- ❖ ALL your best friends are on the nighttime cleaning crew.
- ❖ When you refuse to leave your office, your boss drags you out and locks you out of your office for the weekend for your own good.
- ❖ When you get home before midnight, the kids call the cops because they think you're a burglar.

---

[35] https://www.ilo.org/wcmsp5/groups/public/---dgreports/---dcomm/---publ/documents/publication/wcms_316450.pdf

Chapter 15
BE HERE, NOW
There's No Time like the Present Moment

THESE THREE LITTLE WORDS, "Be Here, Now," is a mantra I try to live by. When I feel myself not being fully present in the moment, I say these three magic words to myself and instantly bring myself in the present moment, fully engaged.

How often is our body one place and our mind someplace else?

We're sitting in church, but instead of getting closer to God, we're wondering if we left the stove on.

We're watching our kid's soccer game. But when she makes that goal, our mind is finishing that proposal for tomorrow morning's presentation at work.

Or when a friend is bearing their soul to us about a painful breakup, we're wondering how bad the traffic is going to be and how long it is going to take us to get home.

It's not that we don't care about the people in the above situations or what is happening around us. We do care and deeply. It's just that we have so many things going on in our lives, it is often difficult to be fully present in each moment.

We don't realize how much we are missing by being there but not really being there.

Why is dwelling in the past or worrying about the future so much easier than just being present in the moment?

Perhaps we're thinking "things were so much better in the past" or "why did I do such and such in the past?" Or some of us are worrying about what the future will hold for us. "Will I ever meet the right person to fall in love with?" or "Is my money going to run out before I do?"

Often, we spend so much time in the past or the future, we ignore our present-our NOW.

Why is it so hard to live here in the moment?

We all have bills to pay, kids to raise, dinner to plan and cook, and vacations to plan. And women know this better than men. Women are the original multi-taskers. But we can get so caught up in planning, regretting, and worrying about what is going on in our lives that we forget to enjoy our lives. We forget to savor, appreciate, and enjoy what we're doing each and every moment of our life.

Just stop for a moment and try to completely clear your mind. No thinking about what happened in the past or what is going to happen in the future. Try to just be right here right now in the moment. Don't think of anything. Just let your mind be empty with no thoughts. Now there's even an app to help you clear your mind.

Okay. How long were you able to last before thoughts started bombarding you again from every angle?

Five seconds, 10 seconds, 30 seconds? Maybe you made it a whole minute. If so, that's not bad. Most people last less than 10 seconds before their mind jumps either back to the past or forward to the future.

After just a few seconds of complete silence, our minds say, "Okay, that was nice, but now let's get back to business."

- "What time do I need to pick up Billy?"
- "What can I do for dinner tonight that's quick and easy?"
- "How am I going to pay my credit card bill this month?"
- "There's no way I can get Susie those shoes she wants."

- "I wonder if I should buy Amazon before it hits $1,000." (Yes).
- "Do these pants make my butt look big?" (By the way, I'm not sure what the appropriate answer to that question is anymore. In my generation, we were looking for the answer to be "No, they do not." However, for the post-Kardashian generation, apparently the desired response is, "Yes, they do make your butt look big.")

Sound familiar?

How can we learn to live here in the moment when we are so wrapped up in the past and the future?

Middle-aged women are particularly vulnerable to stress because they are sandwiched between concern and care for their aging parents on one side and their children on the other. They must juggle their time and energy to take care of everyone. Finding a quiet moment alone in the present can be difficult.

For the more mature ageless woman, living in the past instead of the present might be more of a challenge. Her stress might be caused by other factors such as having outlived a spouse, close family members or dear friends. Sometimes it might seem easier and somewhat comforting to just live in a happier past time when you were hugging your parents, drinking a beer with your brother, or laughing with your best friend.

While these memories may be a tempting place to hang out, they are the past. And as much as we might sometimes want to, we can't live in the past. And this conflict between the past and the present creates stress. Whether it's because of death, marriage or just geography, sometimes we lose people who are precious to us. We must let them stay there in our past (with the wonderful memories) and we must live in the present.

Another very real danger of living in the past or the future instead of the Now is that it can make you look older.

When you are always dwelling in the past or worrying about the future, it causes stress in your mind and your body, and that stress can cause you to age (almost as much as the sun) at an alarming rate.

While you might think that the effects of stress just manifest themselves mentally, studies show that stress shows itself in your body, and not in a good way. Can living with stress make us look older physically? The answer is yes, stress can make us look old before our time.

Studies have shown that the telomeres in our DNA shorten when we are constantly exposed to stress. And the shorter our telomeres become, the quicker we age and the older we look.

Of course, it is not the stress itself that causes you to age, but your response to the stress. That's why it's important to live in the present and be in control of your thoughts instead of the other way around. You will feel less stressful if you feel in control of your present situation. And if you can control your present, it becomes easier to feel more confident and less stressful about the future.

Be in control of your life by handling stress in a positive manner, clear your mind, control your thoughts, and live fully in the here and now. You'll be stress free, happier and you'll look years younger.

YOU MIGHT BE STRESSED OUT IF:
- ❖ You put the kids in the trunk and the groceries in the back seat.
- ❖ You drop the family's dry cleaning off at McDonalds drive-thru and ask for extra starch.
- ❖ You pop Xanax like Tic Tacs.

- ❖ You proudly show up bright and early for your kid's parent/teacher conference – on Sunday instead of Monday morning.
- ❖ You drop your kids off at the Senior Living Center and your mom at Kiddies' Daycare.

Chapter 16
FIFTY SHADES OF GRAY
There must be Fifty Ways to Find Your Lover

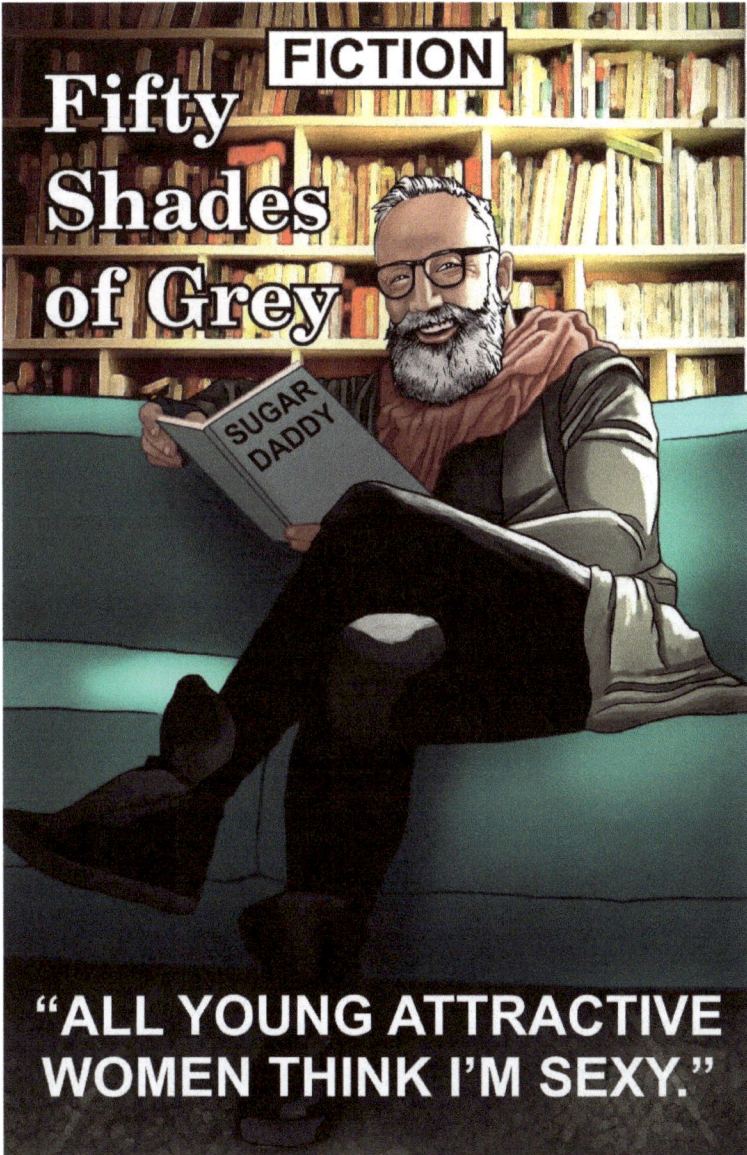

ONE EVENING I WAS STANDING at a mixer for people of a certain age. This guy (probably about 65) comes up to me and says, "Well, you look pretty good. You're not 50, are you?"

To which I did not reply.

Then this guy says, "But what I really want to know is where all the young hot chicks are, like in their twenties. Where are all those young hot women who want to go out with men like me?"

So, I turned to him and said, "Well, you go out the front door here, turn to the left. Oh, you might want to write this down."

He gets out his pen.

"Okay, you turn left, then go about three and one-half blocks. You'll see a bookstore on your left. You go in and go all the way to the back. Look to your right and you'll find them under the section marked 'Fiction.'"

Why a guy would think any girl a third his age would be romantically interested in him I have no idea. I suppose it's just a masculine form of wishful thinking.

Of course, he could always sign up for Sugar Babies/ Sugar Daddies. At least that way everyone knows exactly what they're getting and pay for it upfront.

Men, especially older men, seem to be obsessed with age – not theirs, but ours – women's. I suppose it's an attempt to make themselves feel younger by being with someone younger. But I think it would have the opposite effect. Running around with a twenty-something-year-old guy would certainly wear me out after the first couple of hours (which might be nice).

But seriously, what do we talk about later? And eventually you ARE going to want someone to talk to. And usually, relationships where there is more than a 10-year age difference are not long lived. It takes much more than a physical attraction to keep a relationship alive in the long run. If there isn't a solid basis of similar backgrounds, experiences, and interests on which to build a real connection, the relationship is likely to crumble long before the Silver Anniversary can be celebrated.

Dating after you've hit the half century mark can be challenging for women. Whether you're single, divorced, or widowed, getting back out in the dating world can be a bit tricky. All the support systems and contacts you had the first time around are most likely no longer available. It's like starting all over from scratch. But just like the Marines, you're only looking for a few good men...or maybe just one.

However, one advantage daters have today that did not exist in previous generations is the Internet. One certainly has the opportunity to be exposed to many more possible suitors than ever before. Just turn on your computer, select a dating site or two, put in your information, and before you know it, there are men e-mailing you from all over the world.

In fact, there are even specialized dating services, such as Our Time, for people over 50. I know several people who have found their spouses through these kinds of websites.

Please do not feel that you are the only one out there looking for Mr. or Ms. Right. In fact, singles today actually outnumber married people. In 2014, the number of single individuals rose to 50.2 percent. This was the first time that there were more singles than married people living in America, but this number has been rising for decades. In a *CNN* article published August 12, 2010, entitled "Single? You're Not Alone," Linda Petty says[36] that 17 percent of singles are over the age of 65. And I'm sure this number will increase as the Baby Boomers continue to age.

According to the US Census Bureau, in 1950, only 22 percent of the American population was single. In 1976, the

[36] http://www.cnn.com/2010/LIVING/08/19/single.in.america/index.html

single population had risen to 37.4 percent. By 2010, single Americans made up 43 percent of the population. And today, more than 50 percent of the population in America is single.

So, there are plenty of people out there looking for you just as you are looking for them. If using the Internet for dating is not for you, there are plenty of other ways to meet people besides via computer. There are always the old school ways; pre-Internet methods that worked well for years.

I think the best way to connect is by finding someone who has similar interests and background. If you are following your interests and dreams, you will naturally come across other people with the same interests.

There really are at least 50 ways out there to meet your lover.

Perhaps you enjoy snow skiing, water skiing, scuba diving, bodybuilding, art, opera, theatre, book clubs, gourmet cooking, playing the piano, motorcycling, tai chi, beekeeping, wine tasting, beer brewing, playing the guitar, square dancing, tennis, golf, clogging, karaoke, standup comedy, ballroom dancing, coin collecting, biking, hiking stamp collecting, dog breeding, championship cat shows, screenwriting, country line dancing, bird watching, sailing, miniature golf, hot air ballooning, rehabbing houses, listening to jazz, gardening, astronomy, yoga, Star Trek conventions, Star War conventions, boating, flea markets, pottery, ice sculpting, swimming, horseback riding, classic car shows, or old movies.

Whatever your interest, there is someone out there who is also interested in it.

And don't rule out your family and friends to meet new people. If you are still working, your place of employment is the perfect place to meet potential mates. That is where I initially met my partner.

Or even if you are a volunteer somewhere, get to know the other volunteers and the people who work there. Getting involved in a large church group is another excellent way to connect. Joining a gym or a YMCA will automatically put you in close quarters with lots of men. Another excellent way to meet like-minded men is to join your local political party. It doesn't matter whether it's Republican, Democrat, or Libertarian.

While some older men may still be interested in younger women, there are a lot of men out there who find a certain maturity quite attractive. An ageless woman has many advantages over her younger counterpart. As ageless women, we are generally more supportive, less self-centered, more understanding, more stable, better conversationalists, more sophisticated, more independent (financially and emotionally), and less of a "drama queen." These are mostly qualities that manifest themselves with age. Of course, if a woman is truly an ageless woman, she can have these qualities at any age.

While Mr. Right may be out there, women might have to look a little harder than a man. For every 100 single women, there are only 88 single men. Women do tend to outlive men by a number of years. A study done in 2012 by the researchers for the Centers for Disease Control and Prevention found that the average life expectancy for American women is 81.2, years while American men only lived an average of 76.4 years, almost a five-year difference.

In a *Huffington Post* article[37] entitled "Where Are All the Older Single Men?" Renee Fisher writes: "…older single women have long pondered the enigma of the elusive older single male… In an attempt to ferret out older single men,

---

[37] https://www.huffingtonpost.com/renee-fisher/dating-over-50_b_4084398.html

some women have taken to hanging out at the offices of divorce attorneys and urologists."

She warns that it's a losing battle and statistics prove it. "At ages 50-54, there are equal numbers of single men and single women. At ages 60-64, there are close to 2.3 single women to every single man. By ages 70-74, the ratio is 4 to 1."

Fisher then says that "…the last actual sighting of a single man age 75 or above was made in July of 2008, and he was later proven to be an extraterrestrial. Thousands of older women expressed interest in dating him, but after several unsuccessful dates on Match.com, he fled to his home planet."

She concludes by encouraging all older single men to contact her and she will match them with "fabulous, eligible women" for a certain sum of money. For a larger sum of money, she will keep the secret of their whereabouts.

Hopefully your Mr. Right resides on this planet and is out there looking for you just as you are searching for him.

But don't keep looking for "Mr. Perfect." Don't be like the lady who was told she would be granted any wish she desired. She unselfishly asked for world peace while showing the genie a highlighted map of the Middle East. The genie looked at the map and said, "I'm sorry. That wish is impossible to fulfill. I just can't do it."

The genie handed the map back to her and then asked, "What other wish can I fulfill for you?"

The lady says, "Okay, I would like the perfect man. One that is always attentive to me; a man that loves to cook and clean; he never watches football or golfs on the weekend; he prefers long walks on the beach and romantic dinners by candlelight; he loves my mother; he is very wealthy; and he is tall, dark, and handsome.

The genie looks at her for several minutes, then finally says, "Let me see that map again."

There may be no "perfect" man for you but the "right" man is out there.

There is no age limit on love and companionship. Everyone needs someone to share their life with. Don't give up on love no matter what your age. You never know, love could be just around the corner. If you give up now, you might just miss the best relationship of your life.

But don't look too hard. Get on with your life. Ageless women don't "need" a man to make their life complete. You are just looking for that special someone to enhance your already incredible life. Often things in life come to us when we least expect them, when we are focusing on something else. So, get out there and live your life following your interest and your dreams. And before you know it, Mr. Right is likely to just appear in your life one day.

YOU MIGHT BE LOOKING FOR LOVE IN ALL THE WRONG PLACES IF:

- ❖ You have a profile on EVERY dating site on the web from Affluent Asians to Zestful Xenophobes.
- ❖ You'll go out with any guy as long as he has a pulse.
- ❖ You offer to go Dutch on ALL your dates.
- ❖ You sign up for beekeeping classes even though you're allergic to bees (just to meet a guy).
- ❖ You sign up for a dog obedience class, but you don't have a dog (because the instructor is hot).

Chapter 17
"WILL YOU STILL NEED ME, WILL YOU STILL FEED ME WHEN I'M 64?"

THIS QUESTION WAS first asked by Paul McCartney in 1958 when he was only 16 years old. The song was written by the young McCartney for his father's 64th birthday.

Since that time, this iconic song has served as a love song, a happy birthday song, and even as the introductory soundtrack for the hit movie *The World According to Garp*.

Although I'm sure at the age of 16, Paul had no idea what a deep and philosophical question he was asking, it seems to have evolved into something much more than just a light-hearted question.

Today there are only two Beatles left who could address this age-old question, but since McCartney was the one who originally postulated the question, let's look at his love life through the decades.

If we look just strictly at his life at the age of 64, I'm afraid the answer to that question would have to be "No." At this particular age he did not have a happy, loving relationship. At the time of his 64th birthday, June 18th, 2007, McCartney was separated from his then wife, Heather Mills, and going through a bitter divorce, which was finalized a year later.

He did, however, have a long and loving relationship with his first wife, Linda Eastman. They were married for almost 30 years and were rarely apart from one another. Paul, Linda, and their children lived an idyllic life on a rural farm in England. Unfortunately, her tragic death from breast cancer left McCartney a widower at age 56.

But at the age of 68, McCartney seemed to have found a chance at true love once again. He married for a third time, to American heiress Nancy Shevell in 2011, and it seems to be a good match. Apparently, they had known each other socially years earlier, and have a common background.

Well, what about the rest of us?

If finding and keeping a true love is challenging even for someone as rich, good looking, talented and likeable as Paul McCartney, what chance do we mere mortals have? Will we have someone to need, feed and love us at the age of 64?

We all want to have someone who loves us, who we can just be ourselves with and who we can grow old with.

What are the odds? For a first marriage, statistics show that we all have about a 50/50 chance of a successful marriage.

Before I did the research, I thought that second and third marriages would have a much better chance of working because by then people would be older and wiser. Surely they would have learned what went wrong the first time or two and they would make a better partner the next time. However, this doesn't appear to be the case. Apparently, we don't learn from our mistakes and often just carry them with us into our next marriage. We just repeat the same destructive behaviors, we blame our partners instead of ourselves, and we just keep attracting the wrong type of person.

After the first marriage, there are often no children to bind a couple together to stay in a bad relationship for the "sake of the children." In addition, one or both partners often become more financially, emotionally, or domestically independent.

For example, perhaps the woman has achieved some form of financial independence of her own or a man might no longer depend on his wife to take care of all his domestic needs such as cooking and cleaning. Perhaps he learns to cook and wash his own clothes. As both parties become more self-sufficient, there is less of a need to stay together.

For second marriages, the divorce rate goes up to 67 percent. And by the time we've tied the knot for the third time, we have only a dismal 37 percent chance of staying together for the long haul.

I did discover that the divorce rate for those younger than 50 is about twice as high as it is for adults 50 and older. Young adults, however, are putting off marriage until later in life, after they are more established in their careers and have paid off some of the heavy college debt that most students have today.

The median age for marriage for a man has risen from 26.1 to 29.5 (1990-2016).

The median age for marriage for a woman has gone from 23.9 to 27.4 (1990-2016).

College educated adults also have a lower rate of divorce regardless of age. But even so, the divorce rate is still rising.

But then I thought surely divorce rates are lower for people over the age of 50. Surely by then we've got it together and can form long-lasting and happy relationships. However, we Baby Boomers are changing divorce rates, just as we have influenced everything else.

According to a *New York Times* article by Sam Roberts,[38] a half-century ago only 2.8 percent of Americans older than 50 were divorced. In 1990 about 1 in 10 individuals after the age of 50 was divorced. By 2000, that number had risen to 11.8 percent. By 2011, there were more divorced seniors than there were widowed. More than 15 percent were

---

[38] https://www.nytimes.com/2013/09/22/fashion/weddings/divorce-after-50-grows-more-common.html

divorced with another 2 percent separated. Only 13.5 percent were widowed.

According to an article by Renee Stepler[39] in *Pew Research Center*, "In 2015, for every 1,000 married persons ages 50 and older, 10 were divorced, up from only five in 1990."

So the divorce rate for people over 50 doubled between 1990 and 2010. While divorce rates for adults 50 and older have risen sharply over the past 25 years, it has remained relatively stable for this age group since 2008.

According to data from the National Center for Health Statistics and United States Census Bureau, "Among those ages 65 and older, the divorce rate has roughly tripled since 1990, reaching 6 people per 1000 married persons in 2015."

This new sociological phenomenon has been dubbed the "Gray Divorce."

Most of these divorces among older couples are initiated by the woman in the marriage. In a 2004 *AARP* survey,[40] it was found that 66 percent of the divorces of couples over 50 were initiated by the wife.

Many individuals are finding as they reach this stage of their life that they have little left in common with their mate, or they want to go out and pursue their own dreams that they might have sublimated during the marriage.

Perhaps the glue that held the marriage together-factors such as child raising, career building and wealth management-have been accomplished or are no longer relevant. Or perhaps as they are reaching another phase of life, their needs can no longer be met by that person. They are reevaluating their situation and their relationship and are no longer willing to accept less than they need. Or

[39] http://www.pewresearch.org/fact-tank/2017/03/09/led-by-baby-boomers-divorce-rates-climb-for-americas-50-population/
[40] https://assets.aarp.org/rgcenter/general/divorce.pdf

perhaps just the idea of spending a lot more time (maybe 24/7) around that someone after retirement is not that appealing.

Another very important factor and impetus for senior divorces is simply our extended life expectancies. Perhaps the idea of spending another quarter of a century with someone who you're just not that into anymore doesn't seem like such a great idea.

Is this "Gray Divorce" a negative trend for our generation? Not necessarily. In many ways the higher senior divorce rates are indicative of Baby Boomers' evolving lifestyles. We are living longer, healthier, and more involved lives. At the ages of 50, 60, 64 and beyond we are looking ahead at many years of a still productive life.

Another very popular trend for couples over 50 is to ditch the marriage license all together. Instead of challenging the odds of walking down that risky marriage aisle yet another time, older couples are deciding to give living together a try instead.

In fact, the Pew Research Council reports that the number of adults over the age of 50 who have chosen cohabitation over marriage has grown by 75 percent between 2007 and 2016. This is the fastest rate of growth compared to any other age group.

So whether like Paul McCartney, we find our love and a fulfilling relationship at an age other than 64, let's don't give up the search. Romantic love is worth the wait, no matter what our age.

In her article[41] in *Huffington Post* entitled "The Psychology of Loves That Last a Lifetime," Carolyn Gregoire says that the "trifecta of a romantic relationship – intense love, sexual desire, and long-term attachment – can seem elusive, but it may not be as uncommon or

---

[41] https://www.huffpost.com/entry/psychology-of-lasting-love_n_5339457

unattainable as we've been conditioned to think. In long-term partnerships that do succeed, love tends to fade into companionship and a love more akin to friendship than to that of a couple in love."

But life-long romance is possible. In a 2012 study[42] in the *Journal of Social Psychological and Personality Science*, researchers found that 40 percent of couples who had been married for at least a decade or more were still "very intensely in love."

Other factors which tend to bode well for a long-lasting union are keeping boredom out of the relationship by sharing new experiences together, avoiding being too needy by giving your partner their space, having a passion for life outside the relationship, and moving beyond our basic needs to a sense of self-fulfillment.

What was the number one factor that kept long term relationships the happiest?

In numerous University of Geneva studies on compatibility, which predicted long-term romantic love, they found that maintaining a sense of "love blindness" is critical to its survival.

"Love blindness" is described as that magic feeling when you first fall in love, when you can't think about anyone or anything else, when that person can do no wrong. Couples who were able to continue to see each other in that glowing light - as the most attractive, the smartest, the funniest, and the nicest - were the happiest with their relationships.

So, remember what first attracted you to that person and continue to see him or her through that magical lens and keep that love alive through the years. Who doesn't want to be around someone who thinks they're the greatest?

---

[42] https://journals.sagepub.com/doi/full/10.1177/1948550611417015

"Because no matter how cynical we are about the prospect of life-long love, it still seems to be what most Americans are after. Romantic love is increasingly viewed as an essential component of a marriage, with 91 percent of women and 86 percent of American men reporting that they would not marry someone who had every quality they wanted in a partner but with whom they were not in love."

We are no longer staying in relationships just for security or companionship. We are looking to fulfill our higher needs such as self-esteem, self-fulfillment, and self-actualization.

Whereas before we might have stayed in a relationship because we figured that our lives were pretty much over and it wasn't worth the upheaval, today we are taking those risks and making those changes and following those dreams because we know we have a bright future to look forward to.

SOME AGELESS WOMEN WHO HAVE WALKED DOWN THE AISLE MORE THAN A FEW TIMES:

- Demi Moore – married 3 times (once to Bruce Willis)
- Marilyn Monroe – married 3 times (once to Joe DiMaggio)
- "Uptown Girl" Christie Brinkley – married 4 times (once to Billy Joel)
- Jane Seymour – married 4 times (says she isn't in a hurry to get married again and doesn't know if she needs to be married)
- Raquel Welch – married 4 times
- Jacyln Smith of *Charlie's Angels* – married 4 times
- Liza Minelli – married 4 times
- Rosanna Arquette – married 4 times
- Danielle Steele – married 5 times

- Eva Gabor – married 5 times (Eva wasn't as prolific a serial "marry-ier" as her sister Zsa Zsa)
- Jacqueline Bisset – married 5 times
- Joan Collins – married 5 times (says she has found her soulmate and has been happily married for many years now)
- Rue McClanahan – married 6 times
- Lana Turner – married 8 times
- Jennifer O'Neill – married 9 times (now happily married)
- Elizabeth Taylor – married 8 times
- Zsa Zsa Gabor – married 9 times (famous for getting married and divorced and remarried)

YOU MIGHT HAVE GIVEN UP ON TRUE LOVE IF:
- ❖ At your first wedding, you and the groom flip for it since you've only got a 50/50 chance.
- ❖ At your second wedding, you tell two-thirds of the guests they will receive their wedding gifts back after the divorce if their winning numbers are picked.
- ❖ At your third wedding, you tell three-quarters of the wedding guests to just go on home because it's probably not going to work out anyway.
- ❖ This time you just yell out "I DO" as you speed through a drive-thru "church" in Vegas.
- ❖ A week later you drive-thru the same "church" for your divorce.
- ❖ You forget about the piece of paper and decide to just move in together, where you still are living blissfully together 10 years later.

Chapter 18
DO YA THINK I'M SEXY?
Sex, Love, Testosterone and Transgender

I WAS TALKING with someone over 60 the other day about their sex life (for this book). I asked him if people over the age of 50 or even 60 can still have an active and healthy sexual relationship.

He said, "Well, of course, we all know that people over the age of 60 can still enjoy an active sexual life – just as long as we can get cable or Direct TV."

But for those of us who aren't interested in just sitting on the sidelines and voyeuristically participating, there can still be plenty of action in the main ring. In fact, women's sexual desires can become greater as they age, without the worries of monthly periods, birth control, unwanted pregnancies, and the responsibilities of child rearing. There is a certain freedom that has evolved that can result in a more enjoyable sexual experience.

But I'm not sure that sex has to become all that different once a certain age is reached. I'm pretty sure the mechanics of it all are still the same at 60 as they were at 30. It might just take a little longer to go through the motions.

Perhaps for some, male or female, the sexual desire is not quite as strong or as important as it used to be. But it's certainly still there.

It's like the other night when Richard and I went out for a nice romantic dinner. It had been a lovely evening, and when we got home Richard said, "Why don't we run upstairs and make love?"

To which I replied, "Okay, but pick one, honey, I can't do both."

Surveys indicate that more than half (closer to two-thirds) of women over the age of 50 are still sexually active and still have sexual desires. Yet companionship, conversation and friendship do become more important than they were in previous years. And strengthening these qualities in a relationship would only serve to enhance it at any age, young or old.

Who's to say? Maybe sex at 60 is actually better, deeper and more meaningful than the red hot, quick passions of our twenties.

Certainly, if there is a deep love for a partner of many years, there is no emotional reason for the sexual desire to diminish. If anything, this bond can strengthen through the years.

If there is a physical reason that might limit sexual activity, there are several options available, such as testosterone for men or women. Testosterone levels drop dramatically in both men and women after the age of 50. Testosterone is the hormone that controls sexual desire and libido and both men and women can benefit by having enhanced testosterone levels. If more than testosterone is needed, there are other options available.

Of course, there is also Viagra, the "little blue pill," for men.

Other sexual enhancement drugs for men are Cialis and Levitra.

A new drug for women (basically Viagra for women) is also now available. This drug, Flibanserin, has been called the "Pink Viagra" and was approved by the FDA in 2015. It is marketed under the name Addyi. Its aim is to treat lack of sexual desire in women. Unlike Viagra, which increases blood flow to the genitals, Flibanserin changes a woman's brain chemistry by increasing dopamine and regulating serotonin levels. While the drug has shown promise in increasing women's libido, it does have some potential side effects if not used properly. Also, the drug must be taken daily.

The major restriction is that the pill cannot be taken with alcohol. So the usual romantic candlelight dinner and a bottle of wine would have to be replaced with a bottle of sparkling water, otherwise you might end up with dangerously low blood pressure causing fainting or even unconsciousness and miss out on the evening altogether.

Continued research is being done on other alternative drugs addressing women's sexual libido that might prove effective but less restrictive.

A Dutch pharmaceutical company called The Emotional Brain has shown results with two drugs called Lybrido and Lybridos, respectively. Both drugs contain testosterone.

Lybrido works like Viagra by increasing blood flow to the genital area, while Lybridos contains an anti-anxiety drug called buspirone. Both drugs are meant to be taken on demand up to three hours before needed.

Another very promising drug women might want to be on the lookout for is called Bremelanotide. It activates receptors in the brain to stimulate sexual thoughts and desires. Apparently female rats love it, being four times more likely to initiate sex after exposure to the drug. Sounds like it's worth a shot to me.

Some advantages Bremelanotide has over other products is that there is no alcohol restriction so you can still enjoy that romantic bottle of wine AND have a romantic interlude in the same evening. (But please consult with your doctor about the alcohol to make sure). Also, Bremelanotide does not have to be taken daily. It can be taken on demand in as little as 30 minutes before needed and can last up to six to eight hours.

The initial method of ingestion was a nose spray, which would have taken it straight to the brain center. However, there were high blood pressure problems with this method, so I am not sure exactly how the drug will be produced and marketed.

Palatin Technologies, the company behind this new drug, has partnered with a company in China to distribute their drug there. They also have signed an agreement with AMAG Pharmaceuticals giving them the rights to develop and commercialize Bremelanotide in North America.

Bremelanotide seems like an excellent option for women although I am not endorsing any of these drugs or treatments. However, it's certainly worth a conversation with your doctor and maybe your stockbroker.

So, with all the options available to us today there really is little reason that both men and women cannot continue to enjoy an active and happy sexual life well into their future years.

In fact, more money is being spent on breast implants and Viagra than on aging research. By the year 2040, there should be a lot of elderly people running around with "perky" appendages. I just hope by then everyone has a recollection of what to do with them.

While some things about sex may always stay the same, sexuality on a societal level has certainly gone through some drastic changes in the last few decades.

Even though the first oral contraceptive was approved by the FDA back in 1960, it wasn't made available in the United States until 1965, and then only to married women. It wasn't until 1972 that the birth control pill was made available to all women in the United States. This convenient method of birth control brought about a sexual revolution for women in the late '60s and '70s.

Another change is the nature of relationships. If we were discussing marriage or living together, we were talking about a man and a woman. Today this is no longer the case. A relationship can be between two women or two men. Same-sex marriage is now legal in many states throughout the U.S.

I recently saw a television commercial with the usual tagline "Diamonds are Forever." Two women were shown on camera laughing, having fun, and then they kissed. Then the advertising line, "Tell Her You'll Always Be There" came across the screen.

I suppose everyone has the right to be exploited by the diamond industry.

Of course, having a different sexual orientation isn't a new thing. Almost 30 years ago I discovered that women can be very interested in other women. I had a very short stint playing college basketball and numerous other opportunities to be exposed to different sexual possibilities. It wasn't my thing, but I respected their choices and they respected mine.

Today the choice of one's sexual orientation is much more accepted than it was then. In fact, it was about that time the movie *The World According to Garp* with Robin Williams came out in theatres. The movie was way ahead of its time and apparently very prophetic.

John Lithgow played a NFL football player who had decided he wanted to be transgender. He dressed as a woman and was considering gender reassignment.

At the time, I remember thinking that the whole idea was way over the top. It just didn't seem likely, at that time anyway, that a very masculine professional football player would choose to be transgender.

Fast forward 30 years or so, and Bruce Jenner, one of the most accomplished athletes ever and an Olympic winner, announces that he will now be Kaitlyn Jenner. He was in his sixties when he made this announcement.

What a difference a few decades can make.

I truly cannot begin to imagine what it must be like to feel one way on the inside and be something else on the outside, to be in the wrong body.

I have a friend who is transgender. He had asked me what I thought about him going through gender reassignment. At the time, I tried to discourage him because I was afraid of how others might treat him.

Of course, I had no idea how strongly he felt about it and he made the decision to have a complete gender reassignment. Even though he had some serious complications during surgery, the entire process was successful.

Today she is quite happy with her choice. The last time I saw her she was wearing a long blonde wig, a short red dress, and driving a hot red sports car.

YOU MIGHT NEED TO SPICE UP YOUR SEX LIFE IF:
- ❖ You think June Cleaver is Hot! (It's the Pearls).
- ❖ You think Ward Cleaver is Hot! (I have no idea why).
- ❖ You think Eddie Haskal is Hot! (You need serious intervention).
- ❖ Flipping for who's on top is the most exciting part of your evening.
- ❖ It's only the beginning of the opening credits, and your cork has already popped.
- ❖ The closing credits are rolling, but nothing has yet come to attention much less lift-off.
- ❖ You're the only one in the room.

Chapter 19
FOREVER YOUNG
Do You Want to Live Forever?

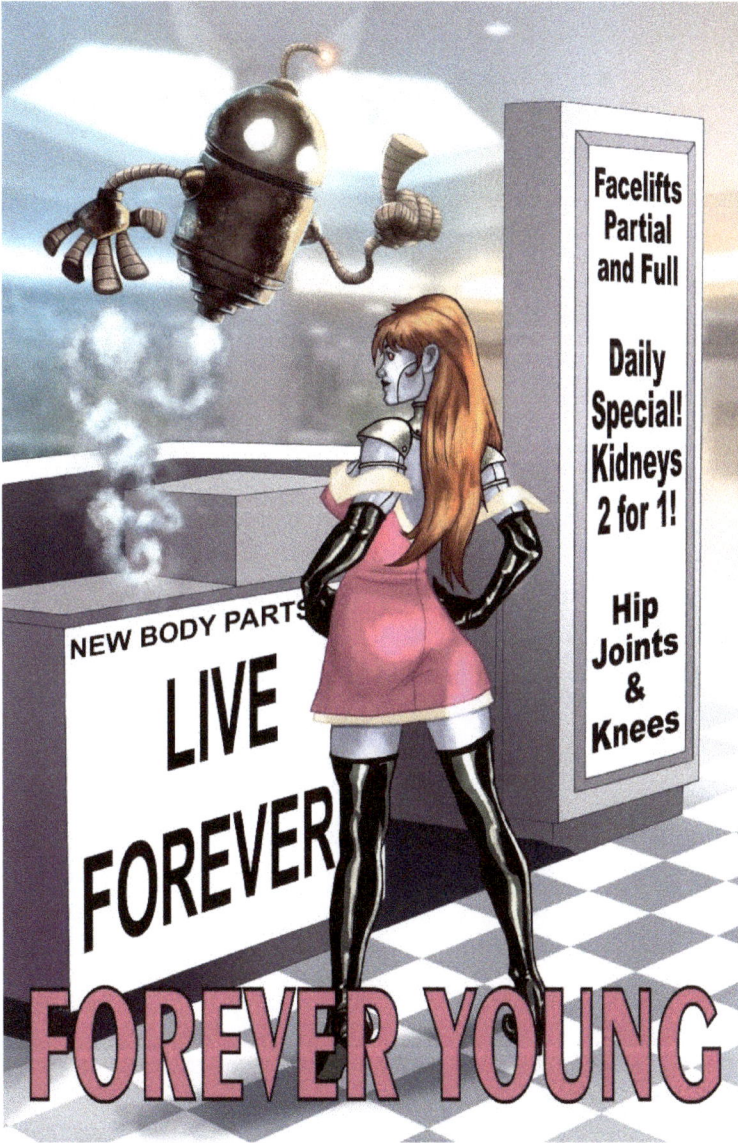

SOMEONE ASKED ME the other day, "Just how old are you?"

I thought about it for a minute then said, "Oh, I'm approaching 40."

He just looked at me somewhat cynically and said, "Okay."

Then I said, "I didn't say from what direction."

We all know that our country is obsessed with aging, or more precisely not aging. No one wants to admit how old they really are; no one wants to look any older as they age; and everyone wants to live forever (as long as they don't look a day over 39). Americans spend billions (with a b) of dollars every year to thwart off the evils of aging.

In fact, according to Neale Godfrey in her article "Use Laughter as a Cheaper Alternative to Plastic Surgery," published in *Forbes*,[43] last year Americans spent $16 million on cosmetic plastic surgery.

That's 290,000 procedures at approximately $4000 each.

Most of that money was spent on Botox ($7 million), Hyaluronic acid ($2 million), Chemical Peel ($1.3 million), and MicroDermabrasion ($800,000).

If you want to go the whole way and get a full facelift, according to the American Society of Plastic Surgeons, that will cost you a little over seven thousand bucks. ($7,048).

Cosmetics, skincare, vitamins, supplements, gym memberships, non-invasive procedures, plastic surgery and even snake venom are our modern quests for that eternal fountain of youth. We think if we can just find that magic potion, cream, diet, or procedure that we can beat the battle of the years. We know it's out there. We just have to find the right combination and we'll be young forever.

[43] https://www.forbes.com/sites/nealegodfrey/2017/09/24/laugh-off-expensive-plastic-surgery/#4fb5a7bb686a

In the movie *The Age of Adeline*, (***SPOILER ALERT***) a young woman has a freak accident when her car crashes into freezing water. Her heart stops completely for a few seconds because of the freezing temperature, and then when she revives moments later, something miraculous has happened. Her aging process has halted. Years go by and she never seems to age a day. Sounds like something we would all be willing to experience, doesn't it?

But even perpetual youth can bring its own unique problems. As people around her begin to change and she stays the same, she is forced to start over every few years and must move to a new city and yet another new group of strangers. She finds it impossible to develop any long-lasting meaningful relationships – even with her own daughter, who continues to age – because she has to watch as others grow old and die while she always remains young.

After a while she avoids getting involved with others at all because she knows she will lose them and doesn't want to go through that pain over and over again.

Her life becomes meaningless until she meets that special someone she can't help but fall in love with. Afraid of the possible implications, she flees, only to fall victim to another auto accident. And miraculously, her aging process slowly begins again. She shares her secret and her life with him, even before realizing that this time she can grow old with her love.

Which would we rather have? A long meaningful life with loved ones surrounding us in which we grow old gracefully, or a number of superficial lives where we stay young forever and decade after decade after decade must start over again?

Although the idea of living in a young perfect body forever, experiencing new people and places might seem tempting, I would imagine it might get tiresome.

Maybe it's just as well. Although that fountain of youth always seems to be beckoning to us just around the next corner, I'm not sure when or even if it will ever be a reality.

Although we spend billions of dollars on anti-aging products, according to Colin Milner, founder, and chief executive officer of the International Council on Active Aging, none of these products can officially be called anti-aging. Why? Because according to the National Institute on Aging, "No treatments have been proven to slow or reverse the ageing process."[44]

Colin's advice? He says you can obtain the energy you need to feel more youthful by getting more sleep, eating a balanced diet, and exercising regularly.

Gary Drevitch suggests[45] in *Next Avenue,* "Also remember that everyone grows older from the moment they're born. Embrace the inevitability of this natural process and the many benefits that come with it."

Woah! Stop! Hold the phone! That sounds like something a middle-aged male engineer would say. Maybe he hasn't heard of Human Growth Hormone, Estrogen, Retinol and Botox.

I'm not ready to give up that easily and I bet you're not either. Maybe we can't actually BECOME younger, but for now I'll settle for looking, acting and feeling younger.

But what if we had the option to do both? What if we could stay young forever AND still have our loved ones and a meaningful life? I'm not talking about just looking young. I'm talking about having a body like Adeline's that would no longer age.

Well, just this year there HAS come some promising news in the anti-aging world. Human trials were done

---

[44] https://www.icaa.cc/media/press2014/graywashing.htm
[45] https://www.nextavenue.org/we-now-spend-more-fight-aging-fight-disease/

which entailed removing senescent cells or "zombie" cells from the body. These cells, which are not dead but too injured to repair themselves, cause many of the characteristics seen in aging.

Researchers used a drug combination of Dasatinib plus Quercetin (a natural substance found in berries) to "clear out" these senescent cells.

While the process did not help with the treatment of a particular disease (pulmonary fibrosis); it did, however, show a meaningful improvement in the participants' physical function. Their physical abilities improved in the following areas: walking speed, getting up from a chair, and various other physical functions.

In another related study, a mild antibiotic called Azithromycin also showed promising results of eradicating these senescent cells. Of course, this is just the beginning of the research and testing, but these results do show real promise of helping to treat and erase many age-related diseases.

Or, better yet, what if we could just transfer our consciousness out of our old worn-out body into some kind of humanized robotic body? Is that possible? If it were, would you sign up?

Well, before we debate the pros and cons of trading in our physical body for an artificial one, let's look at a few less drastic measures that might keep us looking forever young.

HORMONES
One subject we haven't discussed so far is whether to take hormone replacements.

"An Estrogen a Day Keeps Old Age Away." As most of us know, by the time we're approaching 50, we are beginning to feel the first signs of menopause. The most obvious signs of menopause are night sweats and hot flashes. I'm not really sure why they call them "night" sweats because they can and do show up any time of the day or night.

One minute you're discussing something important in a business meeting, eating dinner in a romantic restaurant, or just sleeping soundly. All of a sudden you literally feel like you are on fire from within. Then you break out into a voracious sweat. It is very unpleasant and always comes at an inconvenient time.

So what is happening? You are losing the estrogen and progesterone that you have always had in your body up until now. And you are losing it very quickly.

What can you do about it? For years you had two choices: either tough it out until the transition is complete and your hormones, mostly estrogen, are depleted, or take traditional hormone replacement therapy. These hormones are derived from pregnant mares and then given to humans. I don't know about you, but I did not care for either of these choices.

My hot flashes were numerous and severe, and I did not want to just wait for them to eventually stop. (Of course, some women never even have hot flashes, but most of us have to deal with them).

The other option was to take the estrogen derived from horse urine, and to me that just did not seem right or natural or healthy, so I refused to take the "traditional" estrogen replacement.

Then I discovered Bioidentical Hormone Replacement, which is derived from plants.

This seemed like a much better option to me. However, my doctor at the time refused to write me a prescription for the bioidentical ones because he said they were not scientifically proven. Yet he was more than happy to give me a prescription for the other "synthetic"ones. Needless to say, this doctor is no longer my doctor.

I found a female gynecologist who was willing to go the bioidentical route with me. She has since retired and now a female nurse practitioner prescribes them for me.

Just a few years after all this, the American Medical Association came out saying that a study assessing the dangers of cancer and estrogen replacement was very high. They encouraged women to stop taking traditional hormone replacement, making me very glad that I had not given in to my first doctor's suggestion.

They did not do a study on the bioidentical hormones, but since then, limited studies have been done using bioidentical hormones, and no correlation between the bioidentical hormones and cancer was discovered.

I imagine further studies will be conducted by independent groups to evaluate the long-term effects of bioidentical hormones, however, I'm sure that the American Medical Association and other groups or drug companies will not bother because it is not something they can bottle and sell to you.

Bioidentical hormones are made by a compounding pharmacy and your body determines how much estrogen and progesterone you need.

I am very happy taking my bioidentical hormones and plan to continue them indefinitely. They truly do make me feel younger. Whenever I have a delay in refilling my prescription and go for a few days without them, there's such a difference in the way I feel. It's like all of a sudden, my joints get stiff and sore, and I just feel older.

Estrogen to me is like oil for your car. It's a great lubricant and your car won't go far without it. Estrogen is also needed to keep a plumpness to facial skin.

Usually, the estrogen and progesterone are prescribed together and can often be taken in the same tablet or pill. Testosterone supplementation is also beneficial for sexual libido, energy, and memory.

These bioidentical hormones can be taken orally by capsule, inserted inside your skin, applied as a topical patch, or taken by tablet sublingually. I prefer the sublingual tablet. You just pop it into your mouth before you go to bed and within seconds it has dissolved. It's easy, quick, and effective. Just like that, no more hot flashes!

If you're interested in bioidentical hormone replacement, you will need a prescription from your doctor and then you will need to find a compounding pharmacy to make them for you.

SKINCARE PRODUCTS AND COSMETICS

Every day we are hearing more and more stories about how what we put on our face, skin and hair can negatively affect our health. For years we have been using products unaware of what is actually in them and how these ingredients can cause problems. As mentioned previously, a new study came out suggesting that women who dye their hair regularly may be more likely to develop cancer. There are chemicals in our hair dye, soaps, creams, and moisturizers.

But today women are beginning to take a closer look at what we are putting in and on our bodies. Many of us would prefer more natural and organic ingredients. Another problem many of us have is a sensitivity to smells.

That "fragrance" in our products can actually be disguising some very unhealthy ingredients. It is very difficult to find a true fragrance-free product.

Although I am not endorsing any of these products, here are just a few skincare lines that are organic or hypo-allergenic or are advertised as being more of a natural product:

- Cetaphil
- Aveeno
- Neutrogena

- Rodin-Fields (Creators of Pro-Activ, now have anti-aging and sensitive skin lines)
- Suzanne Somers (organic)
- Aubreys (organic)
- Nature by Canus (goat's milk – canusgoatsmilk.com) – (Please contact them and ask them to bring back their cleansing milk and facial scrub. Best stuff ever)
- Complex 15
- System-41
- Marcelle
- Cliniderm
- Eminence (organic)
- Consult Beaute

If after you've tried natural and other topical treatments and still feel the need for a more sculpted appearance, let's look at some alternatives to the standard facelift.

PROCEDURES
If you're not ready to lay out that $7,000 plus for a facelift and aren't too crazy about going under the knife to find that promise of youth, there are several other, non-surgical options that are not nearly as invasive, that are safer, easier, and cheaper. Although I must warn you that even most of these procedures are not cheap.

Apparently, beauty is neither cheap nor painless, but it seems to be worth it for most of us.

Here are a few procedures you might want to consider:[46]

DERMAL FILLERS
- Juvederm Voluma XC is a gel that's used to lift skin at the cheekbones, smooth crow's feet, pad sunken spots. Also used on the "parentheses" lines that run

---

[46] https://www.prevention.com/beauty/a20467526/anti-aging-procedures/

from the nose to the corners of the mouth. The results are immediate. The cost is $1,200 per injection

- Restylane Silk is a hyaluronic acid gel that's used to plump lines and fill in vertical lip lines. Much better than the older silicone injections that gave the over-plumped "fish" look. Results are immediate and last up to 6 months. Cost is $800 per injection.
- Belotero Balance is a hyaluronic infused gused to tone fine lines in the corners of the mouth and the eye areas. Much better than the previous Botox injections, which gave that stiff expressionless and frozen look. Absorbs naturally into the skin after about six months. Results are immediate. Cost is $800-900 per injection.

ULTRASOUND & RADIOFREQUENCY ENERGY

- eMatrix is a fractional resurfacing using radiofrequency (electrical) energy to help repair sun damage such as age spots, and smooth wrinkles and firm loose skin. It's beneficial in helping collagen to regenerate, and better than the previous Fraxel or C02 lasers because it works BELOW the skin instead of on the surface. It's like a facelift without the surgery. Results are immediate. One major advantage for this procedure is that it can last up to 10 years. Cost is $500 each session (5) sessions recommended).
- Exilis Elite is a radiofrequency treatment for the neck and jawline that will tighten and contour loose skin. Better than Thermage treatments. Thermal heat goes into deep layers of skin and stimulates collagen production. 2-4 treatments usually needed, and it lasts up to two years. Costs $600-$800 each treatment.

- ThermiRF is a radiofrequency skin tightening device that uses radio waves to melt fat tissue and tighten loose skin on the back of the arms. The procedure and device work under the skin. Results are immediate. The cost is $4,000.
- ThermiSmooth is the same procedure as ThermiRF, except the device goes on TOP of the skin. Three sessions are needed. Cost is $300 per session.
- UltraShape System is a body shaping treatment using non-invasive ultrasound energy to target and break up fat cells in the stomach, butt, and thighs. Much easier and safer than the old liposuction surgery. Two-to-three-inch reduction in 2 weeks. Cost is $1,400 each procedure, and 3 sessions usually recommended.

LASERS & NEEDLES, OH-MY
- DermaPen is a micro-needling pen (FDA approved) that uses super fine needles to stimulate collagen production. Used to work to eliminate fine lines, acne scars and age spots, and improve skin elasticity. Preferable to older method of Dermabrasion (used tiny crystals to scrape off layers of skin), which was much more invasive. Results shown in a few hours to days. Cost is $500 each session and 6 sessions are recommended (varies).
- Regenlite Transform Laser is a treatment used to erase acne scars. Does not use heat, so doesn't harden skin, and give it that "leathery" appearance like previous treatments. The cost is $900 each session and 5 sessions are the average (varies).
- VBeam Perfecta is a pulsed dye laser that uses intense but gentle bursts of light to destroy blood vessels or pigment spots. Used to treat facial redness and blotchy appearance caused by Rosacea, acne

scars, or broken capillaries. The cost is $300-$400 per session and 3 sessions are needed.

- One of the newest procedures I've heard of is "The Vampire Facelift". It is a non-surgical procedure with no down time. I assume it is called "Vampire" because part of the procedure is to draw blood (from your arm, not your neck). Then PRP -Platelet Rich Plasma is combined with hyaluronic acid fillers. After being processed, the fluid is injected into the face and new tissue growth is generated.

We may not be able to "stay young" forever, but with so many possibilities available to us, we should be able to "look young" for a very long time.

YOU MIGHT BE PLANNING ON LIVING FOREVER IF:
- ❖ You already have your cryogenics cubicle paid for (you splurged for the full body option-good choice).
- ❖ All your ancestors are centurions.
- ❖ Your great grandmother was rumored to be Queen of the Vampires.
- ❖ You think, "If they can make a Rumba work autonomously, then what's taking them so long to get around to humans?"
- ❖ You have volunteered to be the first human/robot hybrid.

Chapter 20
TOP OF THE WORLD
Woman's search for meaning

WE'VE COME A LONG WAY in our quest for that elusive fountain of youth. We've talked about a myriad of ways to keep our physical bodies young and vibrant. We've discussed how important it is to keep our dreams alive and enjoy our lives. We've examined our career paths and various ways of investing and making money. We've looked at dating, marriage, divorce, and love.

What are we still searching for?

What if, as ageless women, we have all these things - our basic physical needs have been met, we feel safe and secure in our environment, we belong to a group of family and or friends, and we even feel a sense of accomplishment in our lives, whether at work and/or at home. We have more than enough to survive physically; we have a house, we have a family, and we even have a good job and respect of our peers.

What more could we possibly need?

Does all this give us that sense of satisfaction and fulfillment that we are looking for? While all these things are important and a necessary manifestation of our development, have we gone as far as we can? Is there still something that we feel the need and the desire to fulfill? Could there be more to our lives?

If we want to understand where we are going, we must first look at where we have been. To look at what we have done with our lives up to this point and why.

According to Abraham Maslow[47] we all have the same needs and desires. Some individuals are just on a higher or lower level of fulfilling those needs and desires.

For example, a homeless person probably has different priorities than a billionaire. I'm not implying that either one's is better or worse, just different.

According to Maslow, there are five levels of needs, which we go through in our lifetimes. This hierarchy is referred to as "Maslow's Hierarchy of Needs."

The First Level – Physiological – is the lowest level and deals with our basic survival needs. These needs would include making sure we have enough food to eat and water to drink. Also having some type of roof over our head and shelter where we can sleep is a basic need. Without food, water and shelter we are not going to be able to advance to any of the higher levels of fulfillment.

In America, this would seem to be something all of us would have attained by now. However, there are thousands of homeless and hungry people in our country who strive to fulfill this need every day. And in extraordinary circumstances, such as natural disasters, these physiological needs become very prominent.

As I'm writing this, I'm watching the news as Hurricane Harvey has deluged Texas with a horrific record rainfall that has caused massive flooding. Houses and automobiles are submerged, and thousands of people have lost their homes. Many of these houses are in areas that were not flood prone, and I'm sure they never thought this could happen to them. Within a few hours their needs have changed drastically.

In these types of disasters, we see just how important our physiological needs become. The most important thing

---

[47] https://www.simplypsychology.org/maslow.html

now for these victims is getting clean water, hot food, and a place to sleep.

Although these types of disasters make the physiological needs paramount in the short term, it also helps define what is most important in people's lives. Possessions become a secondary concern to the safety and well-being of family members, friends, and neighbors.

You'll often hear a comment such as, "Well, the house is gone, but we're all okay. That's all that matters."

When everything else is taken away, it gives you the opportunity to see what is important in your life.

The Second Level – Safety and Security. At this level individuals are looking first of all for physical security. We want to live where we know we are not going to be attacked by predators or have to fear for our lives. We need physical safety for ourselves and our families. We want to be able to protect ourselves and our families from outside influences. Besides our physical safety, it is important for us at this level to also be able to protect our property, such as our home.

The Third Level – Love and Belonging. By the time we have reached this level, our basic needs have been met. We have food, water, and shelter. We also feel that we and our family are safe and have security. Now we are free to move forward to the next step of fulfilling that need to belong to something greater than ourselves. This is when we start families and cultivate friendships. We want to be part of a group; not alone. We become involved in social groups and activities. Perhaps we join a religious organization or become a member of a local church. We fulfill this need for belonging by joining with other individuals.

The Fourth Level – Self-Esteem. As important as being part of the group was in the third level of love and belonging, in this next level, we begin to want to be more than just a part of the group. We want to be and feel special.

We want to feel that what we contribute is important and appreciated by the others. We want to know that our contribution is valued. We want others to respect us and to show us that respect. It is important for us at this level that others recognize our unique achievements. Perhaps at this level we would actively be looking for that next promotion. We have become self-confident of our abilities, but we want this confidence reinforced by others.

The Fifth and Highest Level – Self-Actualization. At this level we have gone from our most basic needs to our most complex. By this level, we have acquired a sense of who we are and perhaps what our purpose is in life. We have learned a nonjudgmental acceptance of others, whatever their beliefs. Others' status, or even our own, is not important to us as we see all individuals on the same path at varying progressions. We are not interested in impressing other people at this stage of our evolution. Other's views and opinions of us do not influence our actions.

Finding a way to give back to others is often important to individuals at this level. At this level, finding a means of self-expression becomes a very real need. Finding some way to express oneself in a creative way becomes paramount. Perhaps an individual at this level would paint, write, act, direct, sing, counsel others, or create a new foundation or charity. Whatever potential is still left in the individual, he or she would feel the need to fulfill it and express it. There could also be a spiritual awakening or enlightenment at this level.

How do we know which level of needs we have attained and which one we are striving for? That is up to each person to decide, and I think on some level we know what our greatest needs are.

However, as I mentioned with Hurricane Harvey, these needs can change from day to day or year to year. A hurricane, a flood, an accident, a mugging, a theft, a promotion, a firing, a divorce, or death could drastically change one's priorities and thereby one's needs. But in the long run, I think we are all looking for that self-enlightenment or self-actualization.

Remember in Chapter 6 about "Going Your Own Way" when we talked about Julia Roberts showing up at a gala event dressed in white when everyone else was dressed in black? Also think Reese Witherspoon in *Legally Blonde* when she shows up at a Halloween party dressed in a risqué bunny costume and no one else is in costume. What would a fully self-actualized ageless woman do in such a situation?

1. Is she horrified and runs home to change to "appropriate attire?"
2. Does she just go home and not come back?
3. Does she curse the people who wrongly told her it was a costume party and swear to get even?
4. Does she feel uncomfortable but stays anyhow?
5. Does she say "Who Cares?" and has a great time anyway?

   OR

6. She doesn't even notice she's the only one in costume?

Chapter 21
STAIRWAY TO HEAVEN
Women Seem to Have a Step Up On the Next Life

ACCORDING TO COUNTLESS SURVEYS conducted throughout the years, women have always been found to be more religious and more spiritual than men.

Perhaps it's because women just understand God's plan more than men.

It's like when your husband looks at you and says, "How could God have made you so beautiful and so dumb at the same time?"

And you turn to him sweetly and say, "Well, let me explain it to you, dear. SHE made me beautiful so you would be attracted to me AND She made me dumb so I would be attracted to you."

In a recent study, six religious groups were surveyed including Christians, Muslims, Buddhists, Hindus, Jews and the religious but unaffiliated group.

Christianity is the largest religion in the world, comprising 33 percent of the world's population, about 2.5 billion people. Approximately 75 percent of Americans are Christians. Christian beliefs include one God, a Heaven, and a Hell, and that Jesus Christ is the son of God. Also, it accepts that the Bible is the written word of God. The three largest branches of Christianity are Catholic, Eastern Orthodox and Protestantism.

Islam is the world's second largest religion and the fastest growing. Approximately 23 percent of the world, 1.5 billion people, are Muslim. Only about 1 percent of Americans are Muslim. Islam teaches that there is only one God-Allah, and Muhammad is God's messenger. The Quran is the Scripture of Islam. Islam believes in an all-powerful God who will dispense final judgment to the righteous who will be allowed into Paradise or Jannah and the unrighteous will receive their punishment in Hell.

Hinduism is the third largest and considered by many to be the oldest religion. About 15 percent or 1 billion of the world's population is Hindu. Less than 1 percent of

Americans are Hindus. Most Hindus reside in India and Indonesia. Hinduism teaches patience, compassion, and a belief that no living thing should be harmed. Perhaps best known for its concept of "karma," that all actions have consequences.

We're all familiar with Karma, at least the American version. It's when your husband leaves you for his slutty secretary. You get the house and the Mercedes. Three months later your husband loses his job, and they end up living in her parent's cramped and musty basement. Now that's Karma!

The Hindu's ultimate goal is Moksha, which means freedom or salvation.

Buddhism is the world's fourth largest religion. Ten percent or about 500 million people practice Buddhism. Buddhism can be found almost exclusively in the Asia-Pacific region. Only about 1 percent of the American population, mostly in large urban cities and in California, are Buddhists. Buddhism is based on the teachings of Buddha and include practicing meditation, compassion and renouncing craving and attachment to worldly things. The ultimate goal is the attainment of Nirvana.

Judaism accounts for about 15 million people worldwide. It is one of the world's oldest religions. A little more than 2 percent of the American population is Jewish. Judaism teaches a God who will reward the good and punish the wicked. Prayer is a very important part of Judaism. The Hebrew Bible is called the Torah. The word for a Jewish Heaven is Shamayim.

The Mormon religion of the United States is about the same in size as the Jewish religion, approximately 2 percent or about 14 million people, and is the fourth largest religion in the United States. It was founded by Joseph Smith. Almost one-third of Mormons live in Utah. Most Mormons are women, making up 56 percent of the church's population. More than three quarters of all Mormons are married.

Mormons believe in the Bible and their religious text, the Book of Mormon. Mormons believe in three heavenly kingdoms, in which almost everyone can find eventual salvation. These are the celestial, terrestrial, and telestial kingdoms. Your actions on Earth decide in which kingdom you will find yourself.

Besides a belief in a Heavenly Father, Mormons also believe in a Heavenly Mother, who is the mother of human spirits and the wife of God the Father.

I find this particular belief very appealing and seemingly somewhat progressive.

In all these religions, no matter the belief or language, the studies all revealed the same thing; women were more religious than men.

In the *Pew Research Center* study[48] conducted between 2008 and 2016, women (of all religions) were found to be more devout than men with 83.4 percent for women versus 79.9 percent for men. That equates to almost 100 million more religious women than men worldwide.

Being more religious equates to being affiliated or identifying with a certain religion, more likely to believe in God, more likely to believe in Heaven and Hell, a belief in Angels, praying more often, attending weekly church services, and expressing that "religion is very important" in their lives.

This religious gender gap is even more prominent in the United States. According to this same Pew Research study, almost two-thirds (64 percent) of American women pray daily while less than half (only 47 percent) of men pray each day.

---

[48] http://www.pewforum.org/2016/03/22/the-gender-gap-in-religion-around-the-world/

Twenty-one percent of Americans, which includes both men and women, have no religious affiliation whatsoever. Yet men are more likely at 24 percent versus 16 percent to claim no religion.[49] In the United States 68 percent of atheists are men.

Whether women are inherently more religious or are influenced by their environment is debatable. Social and environmental factors that could possibly influence women into taking a greater interest in religion are: having children who are involved with church activities, having the free time available to contribute to church activities, feeling that the church can provide a sense of belonging and security, or feeling that their church can provide a sense of fulfillment not found elsewhere.

Whether women are naturally more compassionate and kinder, which are considered to be both feminine and religious traits, is difficult to say.

Our culture and social norms also greatly influence what roles we play in society. It is interesting to note that women who work outside the home report a lower level of religious involvement than those women who stay at home. Of course, this decreased level of commitment could be simply because of having less time available for church activities and having greater responsibilities in other areas.[50]

Another interesting perspective of women's inherent spiritual superiority was made by Mormon feminist, Caroline Kline in December 19, 2011.[51]

---

[49] https://news.berkeley.edu/2013/03/12/non-believers/

[50] https://www.washingtonpost.com/news/wonk/wp/2016/03/30/why-women-are-more-religious-than-men/?noredirect=on&utm_term=.ed23534e3c28

[51] https://feminismandreligion.com/2011/12/19/women-are-more-spiritual-than-men-the-mormon-conception-by-caroline-kline/

(I must admit that first I did not know there were any Mormon feminists. And second, I was most pleased to see that there are. Nice to meet you Ms. Caroline Klein).

Kline says, in what I assume is a bit of tongue-in-cheek humor:

> "In the Mormon tradition, women are often held up to church leaders and members as naturally more spiritual and selfless than men. While it's nice that Mormonism escapes traditional Christian conceptions of a woman's nature being inherently deceptive, seductive, and sinful (these ideas stem from the Eve narrative in Genesis), this characterization of women as naturally spiritual and selfless does present problems for some Mormon feminists like myself."

She goes on to note that women are not encouraged into the priesthood and leadership of the Church as men are because women are already spiritual. Of course, this results in the women having no real leadership in the church thereby leaving the men in charge.

I can't say it was any different in the conservative Christian church in which I was raised (which made Southern Baptists look like hedonists). The men were in charge. Period. The women could teach classes, visit the sick, plan social gatherings, cook potluck dinners, and, of course, clean up afterwards, but any real leadership or management of the church was handled by the men.

Kline also states that this kind of gender "differentiation" paints men and women into separate corners that might not feel comfortable for them, such as a woman who would prefer to work in a high paying job outside the home instead of full-time childcare.

She also feels that the belief in women's greater spirituality is unfair to Mormon men because it assumes that men are "naturally handicapped spiritually."

With ideas like Ms. Kline's, I do believe there is hope for all of us, men, and women. I must say I agree with her; while I know many very loving and spiritual women, I don't think we have the market cornered on "goodness." Women can be just as ambitious, cut-throat, backstabbing and vicious as any man. In fact, even more so. We just express it differently. Instead of starting a fist fight, a woman might start a rumor instead, or make an unkind and untrue comment about another woman.

I know you've heard the comments women make about other women:

- "Where did she get that awful dress?"
- "Those pants make her look fat."
- "Could she wear any more makeup?"
- "She thinks she is so cool."
- "Who does she think she is anyhow?"
- "Yeah, like those are real."
- "I think she's doing your husband."

I think I would prefer to just duke it out and get it over with.

Of course, we as ageless women do not engage in such nonsense. We have enough confidence in ourselves that we don't feel the need to engage in such behavior.

So, whether you believe as the Hindus do, that you'll be back to try it all again, OR as Christians do, that you better get it right this time or else, OR as atheists, that it doesn't really matter because what happens here stays here and this is all there is, OR perhaps you're an agnostic and just can't decide which team you want to bat for.

Or maybe like the old man who was dying, and the priest kept offering him his last rites, saying, "Denounce the devil and his evil ways before it's too late, my son."

The priest kept asking time and again for the man to repent and denounce the devil, but the man would not respond. Finally, the priest said, "Why will you not denounce the devil, my son?"

Finally, the man says, "Well, Father, until I know for sure where I'm going, I think it's best not to antagonize anyone."

What we do know is that you won't be "here" forever. We all move on somewhere. Whether it's Heaven, Nirvana, Shamayim, Jannah, Moksha, another life as a beautiful, reincarnated butterfly, just in the ground, or somewhere a little less pleasant and a lot further South, we all will "meet up" with some version of transition. So, before we think about what happens in the next life, let's take a look in the next chapter about how we handle our spiritual beauty is this life.

YOU MIGHT NEED TO WORK ON YOUR SPIRITUAL SIDE IF:

- ❖ You Haven't Seen the Inside of a Church Since Your Christening.
- ❖ You think philanthropy is something your husband is always doing behind your back.
- ❖ You think the Red Cross is a scam and would never donate a penny.
- ❖ Your favorite character at Christmas is Mr. Scrooge.
- ❖ You think all those annoying homeless people should just find a place to live and get a job already.

Chapter 22
DORIAN GRAY
Beauty from the Inside Out

SO, WHAT DOES IT MATTER what we look like on the inside? As long as we can push, pull, and tug our way into looking good on the outside, right? So what if we're ugly on the inside? It won't show on the surface, will it?

Remember that old saying, "You get the face you deserve by the time you're 40?"

Or is it 50 or 60? Either way, it just might be true. I truly believe that a lifetime of fears, love, hate, disappointments, revenge, sadness, grief, envy, and happiness do show up in our faces. Bitterness, worry, misery, envy, jealousy and judgment seem to etch themselves permanently into our faces and our bodies. And it's not a pretty sight!

On the outside, deep furrows can form between the eyes, wrinkles deepen, and lines appear around the mouth caused by too much frowning. (Smiling is much better for your facial muscles).

On the inside, these negative qualities can fester, causing disease and illnesses such as ulcers, high blood pressure and perhaps even cancer.

So how can we keep our "picture," our "image of self," our "soul" from looking like a Dorian Gray portrait?

Just in case you're not familiar with Mr. Gray, he was the title character in a nineteenth century novel by Oscar Wilde. Dorian Gray was a handsome, innocent young man, seduced by the hedonistic lifestyle of the time. He hurt, cheated, and used everyone around him, but seemed to never suffer any consequences himself. As he grew older, he also never seemed to age.

Later we discover that the "real" Dorian Gray is actually his portrait, which has absorbed and reflected all his ugliness. Instead of a young and attractive man he is hideous, old, bitter, and mean. When he decides that only a full confession of his sins will absolve him, Dorian stabs his portrait, essentially trading places with his painted self, which is restored to its original beauty. Dorian's corruption – and the knife – is transferred to his body, and his servants discover his withered and disfigured corpse, a knife in his heart.

So how can this cautionary tale of Dorian Gray keep us looking young and ageless? Well, unless we have a "magic" portrait like Dorian's hidden in a back room somewhere that will absorb all our banal and evil thoughts and qualities, we will have to learn how to look at life in such a way that brings out the good qualities in ourselves and in others.

Have you ever noticed if you like someone, they have a tendency to like you back? As you see the good in other people and reflect that back to them, they will usually respond in kind. What you give to others is what you receive.

Does everyone hate you, dislike you, make fun of you and talk about you behind your back? If so, it's probably a good idea to look in the mirror first before you blame everyone else. You might just find the culprit there. Maybe they are just giving back to you what you have put out there first.

Find the best in others (even if it's hidden) and they will see the best in you. It's a rare gift to be able to always see the good in others, but it is one you can develop even if it doesn't come naturally. Try it. And don't bother being envious of someone else's life or possessions or appearance.

Don't waste your life wishing you were someone else. Someone thinner, taller, shorter, more curvaceous, richer, who can sing, who has no kids, who has eight kids, who has curly hair, straight hair, bigger boobs, smaller boobs, bigger butt, smaller butt (again, I'm still unsure which is preferable today).

They all have their problems, trust me. Probably more than you. Even though someone may seem like they have everything, everyone wants something they don't have. You really don't want to trade.

Take your life and make it what you want it to be. No one else can. Let your own unique self and your own special beauty shine through.

Have you ever seen someone who was so "good" they just seemed to have an "inner glow" radiating from the inside out? You could just practically "feel" their goodness because it was so strong.

Honestly, I think very few people have this quality to that extent, but I have seen people who do.

My Aunt Betty was like that. She was just so "good" it gushed out of her. You could even feel it over the phone hundreds of miles away. It wasn't fake or forced. I don't think she could have turned it off if she tried. She just always made you feel like you were the most important person in the world, and she truly cared about you.

Evonne, the lady who took care of my parents before they passed away, was like that. She had the most beautiful spirit! I could feel her goodness when I was in her presence. I think I could almost "see" it. It was as if she glowed. Her "Dorian Gray" portrait would have been glorious.

Need a little more motivation for being a good person on the inside? If having a "glow" about you isn't quite enough, just think what that would do for your skin. Every woman I know would love to have glowing skin.

YOU MIGHT NEED AN INNER BEAUTY MAKEOVER IF:

- ❖ You know everyone is always out to get you.
- ❖ Just because you're paranoid doesn't mean that they're not really after you.
- ❖ You often wonder, "Why does everyone hate me?"
- ❖ You know you better get yours before everyone else does.
- ❖ Why are people always picking on me?
- ❖ Why do all the bad things in life always happen to me?

Chapter 23
MAGIC OF THE LAW OF ATTRACTION
You'll See It When You Believe It

WHETHER WE'RE TALKING ABOUT youth, beauty, wealth or just a happy life, we first have to believe in our ability to possess it. We must truly believe it is something we are worthy of possessing. In fact, we must truly believe that it's already ours and all we have to do is accept it into our lives.

It is not something we get by longing for, daydreaming about, or desperately wishing for but is always just out of our grasp. Our belief that it's inside of us is the true magic of creation.

Creation or attraction starts from the inside out, not the other way around. You don't just go out and bring home wealth unless you first have the belief that it is yours to bring home. In the same way, if you don't feel that you are youthful and attractive, no matter what you do, no one else will see the youth and beauty in you.

You must believe in yourself and those qualities you want to possess and project that out into the world. Others will see what you believe and believe it themselves. It's almost like a magic trick with smoke and mirrors.

Have you ever known someone who seems to have all the qualities that you want, and they always seem to get what they want out of the world?

Why is it that some people have all the luck? They win the gene lottery with their good looks, or they're just naturally tall and thin and can get a chocolate cake every day and never gain a pound, or they're funny, or they're Einstein-smart, or they can sing like Adele, or their parents have a couple boatloads of money.

It's like Life said, "Okay, you can come back for seconds and thirds. No problem. Take all you want."

Of course, we're still waiting at the back of the line wondering what's taking so long to get ours. Some people just seem to have all the luck, literally. Yours, mine, and everyone else's. Everything seems to always work out for them. Whether it's good health, a romantic relationship, money, a new car or box seats to the big football game, everything just seems to fall into their laps. While the rest of the world spends their time longing for all these things, these few "special" people just automatically get them. How can this be?

We wanted that new Mercedes too, but we're still driving that 10-year-old clunker with no air conditioning.

And how awesome would it be to watch the game from high atop the stadium while sipping champagne, looking down on the masses instead of sitting next to this fat guy who keeps spilling beer all over my suede shoes?

What do these people have that the rest of us don't? Are they better people? Or maybe they deserve it more than we do. Maybe we just need to work harder and then we'll get all these things, right?

Not really. We all know plenty of people who work themselves to death and never seem to get ahead or get anything they want. And do the "good" people who seem deserving get rewarded by receiving "extra" swag or bling? Not usually.

And we all know plenty of jerks who might be rich but certainly don't seem to deserve their wealth and the finer things in life that they enjoy, and we don't. So why are they driving around in OUR fancy sports car and drinking OUR Dom Perignon and hanging out in OUR reserved seats?

Because they truly believed it was already theirs before any of it ever actually appeared. It was already theirs in their MIND. They just brought it into this plane of existence.

They weren't just wishing these things would materialize. They KNEW they would. They had already claimed them, and you can do it too.

So, whether you're wanting a young, attractive body, a romantic relationship, a successful business, friends, or money, then first picture all these things or events as already happening in your mind. Truly FEEL as if you already have them. Picture yourself in that new convertible with the wind blowing through your hair. See yourself in that box seat with the waiter pouring your champagne. Know that they are yours. Accept them and receive them into your life. Be thankful for them before you see them. Ask knowing that it is already done, and it will be yours.

There is a myriad of people who have written books about the Law of Attraction and how to make it work for you. Some of my favorites are:

- *Ask and It Is Given* by Esther Hicks and Jerry Hicks
- *You'll See It When You Believe It* by Wayne Dyer
- *Becoming Magic* by Genevieve Davis

Getting the Law of Attraction right is the difference between just wishing and wanting and not having versus believing and having your desires and enjoying your life.

For me, the trick (if there is a trick) to the Law of Attraction is to not spend all my time thinking about and wishing for things, but instead to focusing on accepting and receiving those things into my life and being thankful for them BEFORE they appear.

In her book *How to be Wildly Wealthy FAST*, Sandy Forster describes the Universe as a sort of giant warehouse that's filled to the brim with any and everything we could possibly ever want. All we have to do is place our order while continuing to believe that it's going to show up. Then we just wait for our order to arrive. It's not just positive or wishful thinking; you have to truly believe it's coming. It's kind of like ordering a pizza from Dominos. You have faith that it's coming and you're pretty sure you'll see it in 30 minutes or less. But either way, you believe it's coming.

Sometimes the bigger our orders, the longer it can take to deliver. But keep believing.

If you start thinking negative thoughts like, "Who am I kidding? I can't afford that car." Or "Yeah, right, like I'm ever going to even see the inside of those box seats much less watch the game there. I might as well get used to Jimmy Bob sloshing his Pabst Blue Ribbon beer all over me."

When you start thinking thoughts like these, you start attracting exactly what you don't want, not what you really do want. You are in essence cancelling your order for the good stuff and placing a new order for the "bad" stuff.

That order you put in for the red Ferrari, which might have been just weeks away from showing up in your driveway, is marked "Cancelled" and your car is rolled back into the warehouse.

Sandy says you probably don't realize how many times you have ordered and then cancelled that sports car.

Don't give up on that Ferrari or that McMansion or that perfect guy. If you truly believe it is already yours, you can manifest it all into your world.

But do be very careful what you wish for.

You don't want to end up like the lady who found an old lamp in her attic. When she dusted it off, a Genie appeared and granted her three wishes.

The first thing she asked for was to be the most beautiful woman in the world; her second wish was to have all the money she could ever spend; and the third wish was to turn her beloved cat into the most handsome prince around. In a flash, the Genie was gone, and the lady looked in the mirror. She was indeed beautiful. Then she looked down and saw piles of money everywhere. Thrilled, she looked over where her cat had been and saw the most gorgeous sexy man she had ever seen.

He came over, took her into his arms and whispered softly, "Now, aren't you sorry you had me neutered?"[52]

So do be careful what you ask for. You might just get it.

But, hey, maybe the guy who delivers your Ferrari will be Mr. Right. The Universe works in mysterious ways.

YOU MIGHT NEED TO WORK ON YOUR ATTRACTING ABILITY IF:

- ❖ You're still driving around in a '74 Pinto.
- ❖ You're wearing last decade's clothes.
- ❖ You drink your wine out of a box.
- ❖ You live in a sixth-floor walkup with no elevator and no air conditioner.
- ❖ You still live with your mother because you can't manifest a new apartment.
- ❖ You boyfriend is unemployed, ugly and not much fun.

---

[52] http://www.joke-db.com/c/genie/clean

Chapter 24
AGAINST THE WIND
After the Storm Clouds

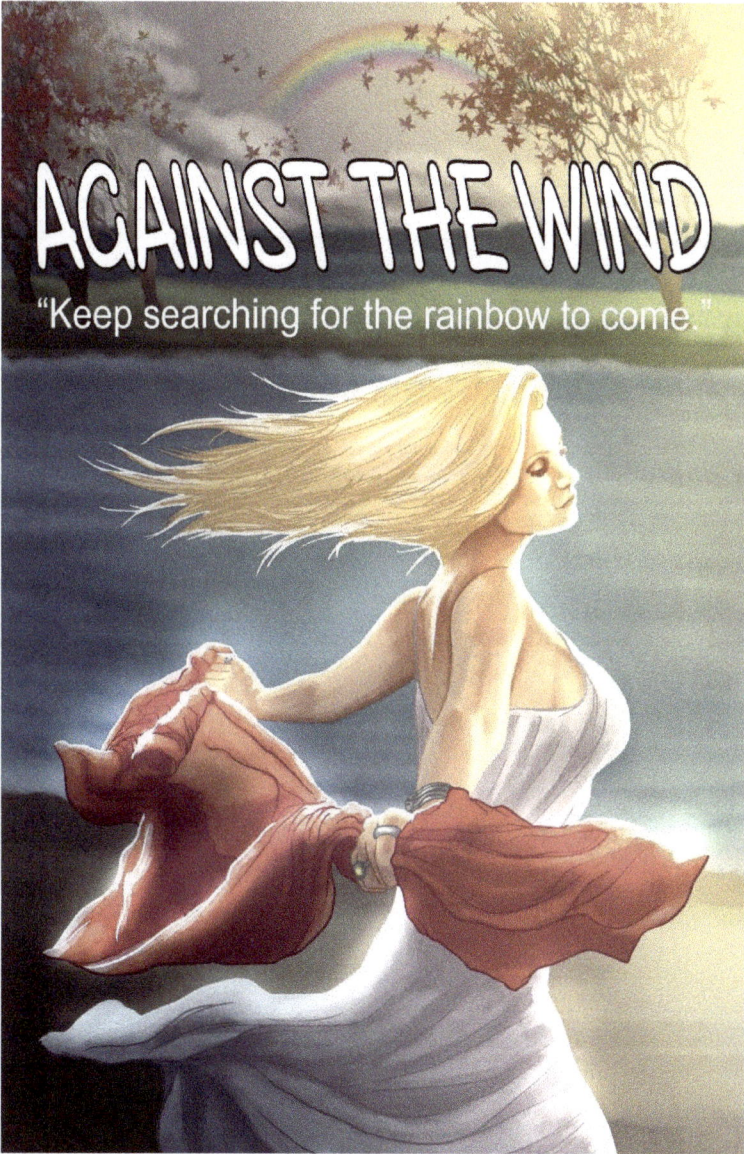

MY GRANDMOTHER ONCE TOLD ME a story about a little old lady who used to live down the street from us who was afraid to leave her house. The entire time she lived on that street my grandmother never once saw her come out the front door. She would have her groceries – and I suppose anything else that she needed – delivered.

She just knew if she left that house something bad would happen to her. Now we understand, of course, that she was suffering from a mental condition called agoraphobia. But back then they just thought she was odd.

She lived by herself in that house isolated and supposedly safe for almost 30 years. Then one day Life came knocking (loudly) at her door as Life has a way of doing. An F5 tornado came roaring through the town, which was unusual because the town had never seen a tornado before or since.

After the tornado had roared through the small town, it became apparent that only one house had suffered any damage. The roof of the house was completely blown away and almost half of the house itself was just gone. As people rushed to the aid of the homeowner, lightning suddenly struck a large tree next to the house. The burning tree slowly fell on the house, setting what was left of it on fire, and the remainder of the house burned to the ground.

The house that had been demolished by wind, lightning, and fire was none other than the house of the little old lady; the house she had so adamantly refused to leave for all those years. Fortunately, she escaped miraculously without a mark on her, but she had no choice than to leave what was left of her house.

Sometimes Life can feel like that. It's like we're always struggling against what Life is getting ready to throw at us next.

By the time you've made it to the age of 50, you've most likely gone through a number of life-altering experiences, not all of them good. Even positive events such as relocating for a new job, going back to school, buying, or building your dream home, retirement or traveling to exotic locales you've only dreamed about can be stressful and challenging. Events such as death, divorce, accidents, unemployment, financial problems, or physical impairment can leave the most optimistic of us unsure of where to turn and can cause some very unpleasant feelings for us to have to confront.

Sometimes these feelings of stress, isolation, grief, anger, abandonment, depression, or grief can seem overwhelming. It all just seems like too much. It all just seems so unfair. Unfortunately, it is unfair. Most of the time there seems to be no reason why things happen the way they do.

Bad things happen to good people. They just do. And sometimes good things happen to bad people.

Most of us know and can appreciate our lives when things are going well for us. However, unfortunately, the storm clouds of Life can show up at our door when we least expect them. And is doesn't matter why they're there, they just are. And it doesn't matter who we are, we're left to deal with the aftermath of the storms in our lives.

Just like the lady who was afraid to leave her house until she had no choice, most of us must take what Life has given us and attempt to turn it into something if not positive at least constructive. We make an effort to rebuild our lives no matter how daunting the task.

I know when my parents passed away a few years ago, I was grief stricken. Even though I was an adult, I suddenly felt like an abandoned and orphaned little child. Everyone says that's the way of the world, the way it's supposed to be; your parents die before you do. But when it happened, it certainly didn't seem natural to me. What seemed natural was that they would ALWAYS be there. It just seemed sad, devastating, unbelievable and lonely. Then the loss of my sister and the separation from my brother came not long afterward.

The nuclear family that I had always derived such strength from was no longer there. Whether I wanted to or not, I had to accept it and try to find a new direction and purpose for my life.

I know a number of women who have experienced the pain of losing a spouse after many years. Some of my friends have even had to endure the unthinkable and unbearable loss of a child or grandchild. There could be nothing more tragic or any pain greater. After losing a child it can seem as if there is no reason to go on or to even get out of bed in the morning. It's like, why bother to do anything?

When we have loss like this, we feel that nothing will ever be the same again. Unfortunately, this is true. Things won't ever be the same as they were.

But whatever storm has happened in your life, you're still here or you wouldn't be reading this book right now. And you're still here for a reason, even though you may have no idea what that reason might be.

You still have a lesson to learn, someone has a need only you can fill, or you still have something special to give the world that only you can give. You are still here for a reason.

My friend who lost her adorable blonde-haired son, has several other children who still need her. That is her reason for being here and going on with her life.

I also have a dear friend who lost her truly "movie-star" beautiful daughter and unborn grandchild in a senseless drunk driving accident. She is still here to raise her other beautiful grandchild and to make a life for her. She is the only person who can fulfill this need. I have been beyond amazed at the strength and grace she has shown in such a tragedy. She and her lovely mother, who is also a big part of their lives, are both here for a reason. They are truly beautiful, ageless women, both inside and out.

So, what does it take to get through the ecstatic highs and devastating lows of our lives and still be standing? How can Life be so wonderful one minute and so awful the next? How can we deal with depression, fears, anxiety, and grief so that they don't overwhelm us? How do we survive the unsurvivable and live to enjoy the wonderful parts of our lives yet to come?

We must first be willing to believe that our lives are still worth living. We must accept that our lives CAN get better in the future. We must be stubborn enough to hold on until we reach a better time and place than where we are now. We must choose to see the positive in our situation, even when it's seemingly nonexistent. We must believe that we are still here for a reason, that our life has a purpose.

As ageless women we know that life is full of both amazement and heartache. Very few of us are going to make it through this life without experiencing both. It helps to have family, friends, and neighbors around you when you are going through life's storms. Don't isolate yourself and try to do it all on your own. There are people and groups out there to support and help you.

Don't give up. Find that reason for which you are meant and keep moving forward, however rough that road may be. Even though you may not get over what has happened to you, just try (for now) to get through it. Unfortunately, we all lose someone if we're here long enough and our only real choice is to keep going.

"Here is a test to find whether your mission on earth is finished. If you're alive, it isn't." (Richard Bach)

And, oh, by the way, what ever happened to that little old lady who was afraid to come out of her house? Apparently, after her house was destroyed and she was forced out into the open, she lost her fear of the outside world and became a world traveler. Last I heard, she was in the South of France traveling with a much younger male companion.

YOUR LIFE MIGHT BE FULL OF STORM CLOUDS IF:
- ❖ Your favorite book is *Les Miserables*.
- ❖ You lived in Texas during Hurricane Harvey (of course, you had no flood insurance).
- ❖ You lived in Florida during Hurricane Irma (again, with no flood insurance).
- ❖ You moved to Puerto Rico right before Hurricane Maria hit (I really think you should move to Kansas).
- ❖ You KNOW that you are always going to be miserable (which, considering your housing choices, might be true).

Chapter 25
IF YOU CAN'T PLEASE EVERYONE
You've Got to Please Yourself

LIFE CAN BE A LOT MORE FUN and perhaps a little easier if we look at it from our own unique perspective. We so often try to live our lives to please other people. We do what they want, what makes them happy and then we wonder why WE'RE not happy. Even though we know we're an octagonal peg, we try to fit ourselves into a round hole to please our husband, our mother-in-law or our boss. But no matter how hard you try, that peg is not going in and it's not going to feel good trying to make it do so.

> "Here's to the crazy ones – the misfits, the rebels, the troublemakers, the round pegs in the square holes. The ones who see things differently – they're not fond of rules, and they have no respect for the status quo..." – Steve Jobs

You were not put here to live up to other people's expectations. You are here to discover your own path and be your own person. You are not here to contort yourself into being who everyone else thinks you should be.

Women are particularly likely to be people-pleasers. Our society teaches women it's acceptable to be submissive and subservient and put others' needs before our own. We're taught that our goals are not as important as others'.

We tend to put our family, our spouse, our co-workers, our church group, our friends, and complete strangers' needs, desires and wants before our own.

No wonder we get burned out, depressed, resentful, and anxious. The last person we take care of is ourselves.

But Life is a lot like the instructions they give you on an airplane – "Put the oxygen mask on yourself first before you place it on your child." If you don't take care of yourself first and be true to yourself, there won't be anything left to give to others.

Be true to who you really are, not what everyone around you expects you to be. Act in a way that reflects who you are and what you believe. Don't mold yourself into others' expectations of you. Express the real you, not just a reflection of everyone else. Otherwise, one day when all the kids are gone and the house is empty, you might not recognize yourself when you have only your eyes looking back at you.

Don't be just a mother, just a wife, just a daughter, just a sister, just a grandmother, just a part of your company, just a part of your church group, or just a part of your bridge club. Be the one and only you that only you can be. Don't wait for others to give you your identity and define and tell you who you are.

Sure, you might be a great mother or the world's best grandparent, but that's only a part of who you are. You might also be the world's best debater, a world-renown chess player, a great sculptor, a hilarious standup comedian, a glamorous model, a bestselling author, or a scientist who is going to find the cure for Alzheimer's.

Who you are is at your core. Deep down you know who that is, and it is not something that can be given to you by others. You truly are the captain of your own life. Don't give away the wheel to someone else, even those you love the most. Show them how to follow their True North by following your own star.

Don't get to the end of your life and wished you had tried for your true dream but didn't because you were so busy trying to please everyone else that you forgot to live your own life. If YOUR dreams aren't important enough for you to try to go for them, then they are certainly not going to be important to anyone else.

How can you expect others to give you support and help you succeed when you don't even take yourself seriously? And eventually you just get tired of being a part of everyone else's lives but never really owning your own.

Have you ever noticed the harder you try to please somebody, the more they demand of you and never really seem to be satisfied? Don't give away your power to someone else, no matter who it is. Demand that they respect you for who you are. Let them know that your wants, dreams, and desires are just as important as theirs and you expect them to respect them. Because you truly cannot, no matter how hard and how long you try, please everyone all the time. Please quit trying to do so. Learn to just say no.

Instead, learn to please yourself and see how much more fulfilling your life can be.

"If you spend all your time living everyone else's lives, who is going to live yours?"

YOU MIGHT BE TRYING TOO HARD TO PLEASE OTHERS IF:

- ❖ You are always the only one up at three in the morning.
- ❖ You've considered using your personal car as an Uber vehicle since you're always out driving all the kids in the neighborhood around anyhow (You might as well get paid).
- ❖ You are always the one the school comes to at the last minute for your special brownies and cupcakes.

❖   You always volunteer to go on the school trip as a chaperone at the last minute when the other parents cancel.

❖   You coach your son's baseball team on Monday, your daughter's soccer team on Tuesday, and the twins' basketball team on Thursday. Then you take your other daughter to ballet lessons on Fridays after you babysit your grandson on Friday mornings. On Wednesday night you teach a Bible class of high school girls. On Saturday nights, you always go out with your husband's work associates, whether you feel like it or not. Sometimes you get to rest on Sundays and have a few minutes to yourself, but only after you sing in the choir Sunday morning and before you go back to the church Sunday night to volunteer as an usher and a greeter.

Chapter 26
I'M AS GOOD AS I ONCE WAS
As Long As…

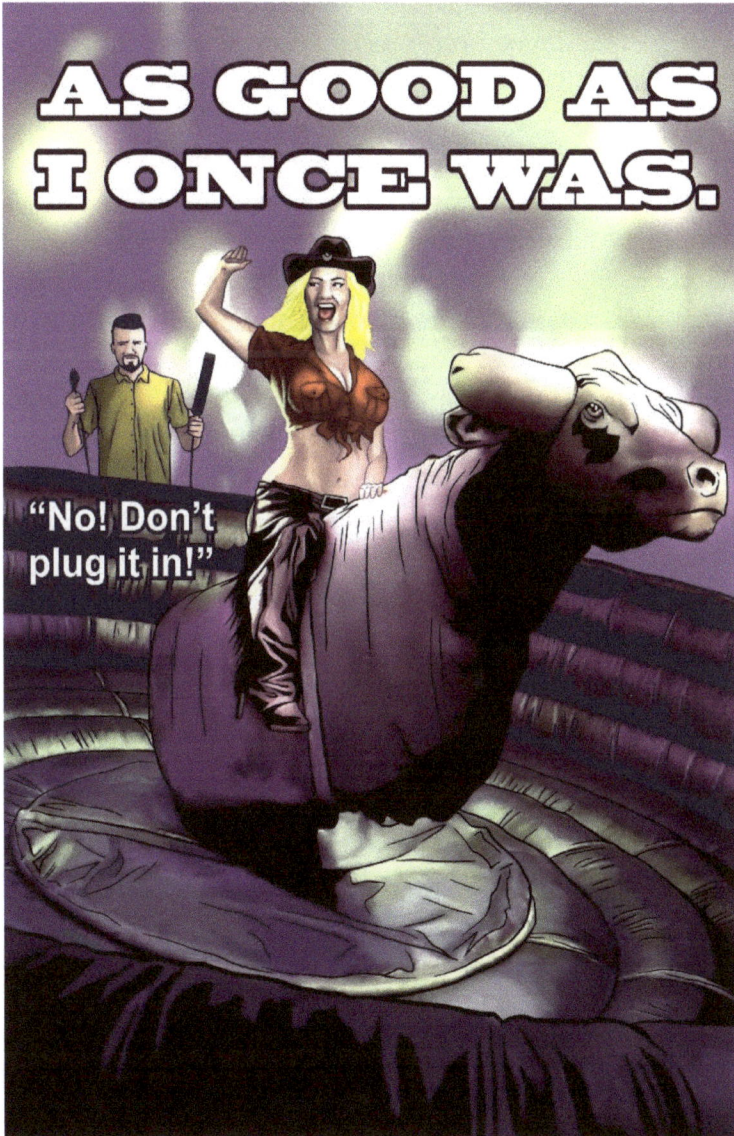

OKAY, SO MAYBE I DON'T look exactly like I did 20 or 30 years ago, but I do still get whistles from construction workers (I suppose the hard hats do restrict their vision somewhat).

And maybe I don't feel the same physically as I did two decades ago. Maybe I can't party all night and work all day the next day. But I can still party all night just as long as I only do it once every two months and can sleep for the next three days.

That reminds me of the older lady (she looked 70-ish) I met when I used to jog by her house during the late afternoon. She would always be sitting on the front porch with a drink (bourbon) in one hand and a cigar in the other. She seemed very spry and active for someone her age. I would stop and talk with her every now and then. One day I asked what her secret was to looking and acting so young.

She said, "Well, Honey, I drink a bottle of bourbon a day, I smoke three cigars, and of course, I can't do without my snuff. And then on the weekends, I usually have one of my boyfriends over to visit."

I said, "Well, you look great. Do you mind me asking, how old are you?"

To which she proudly replied, "I'll be 39 next week."

So maybe partying, drinking, and smoking ISN'T the secret to staying young after all. But, hey, we're not supposed to look and act the same as we used to. And I don't want to spend the rest of my life trying desperately to look like I did in the first part of it. Do we really want to be some kind of Frankensteinian version of our younger selves? I don't. Maybe growing old gracefully isn't such a bad idea after all.

And just think how strange would it be if we never did change? How would you like to look like you did 20 years earlier if you were a senior in college? You would look like you were in kindergarten. Instead of hanging out at fraternity parties having fun, cheering at football games and dating a lot of guys, you'd look like you should be home playing hopscotch, dressing your dolls and coloring in your books. Then later, when you are a young mother or a career woman, you don't want to look like a sorority girl.

When you become a CEO or a brain surgeon or an accountant, you want to look like you have some experience, not like you did 20 years earlier, when you were first starting out.

And 20 years after that, when you're a wealthy, retired beach bum, you don't want to look like a CEO anymore.

Of course, you can look like a Cougar at any age. It doesn't matter if you're in the CEO or the beach bum phase of your life. But it's healthy to move forward in life, whether it's from childhood to adolescence, or adolescence to adulthood and beyond. Each decade has something to teach us. Life is meant to be lived in stages.

Everyone isn't supposed to be 22 or 37 or even 44. In fact, most of the people in the world who are contributing something to society are already well over 40. By the time we get it right, most of us have a few years on us, whether we are male or female.

And what is it with Americans being so darn absurdly, ridiculously, fanatically, and superficially obsessed with age, especially women's ages?

I think we should take a lesson from the Japanese; start actually having a reverence and respect in this country for those of us who have accumulated more years. Not just lip service but a real admiration. We're the ones with all the experience, the brains, the real estate and the money. Be nice to us and maybe we'll give you some free advice and a couple of bucks.

YOU MIGHT BE AS GOOD AS EVER IF:
- ❖ You can still party all night, as long as you can sleep the rest of the week.
- ❖ You can still run a marathon, as long as it's divided into separate sections and different days.
- ❖ You can still put long hours in at the gym as long as it's in the sauna, steam room and whirlpool.
- ❖ You can still get propositioned by the gardener AND the pool boy.
- ❖ You can still ride the mechanical bull at Gilley's as long as no one turns the darned thing on.

Chapter 27
"LET'S GIVE 'EM SOMETHING TO TALK ABOUT"
"How About Us?"

REMEMBER ALL THOSE CRAZY fun things you used to do when you were young? When's the last time you did something like that? Have you become too conservative and sophisticated to have a good time anymore? Do you feel it's just not "proper" at your age to let loose and throw caution to the wind and really enjoy yourself?

Well, it may not be proper but it's also not much fun. Maybe it's time to let your hair down and enjoy life.

Today, women over the age of 50 are not ready to get into the slow lane of life. We aren't done yet and there is no age limit on enjoying life.

What things did you used to do when you were younger, or put off doing because of your responsibilities? Staying up all night just talking, taking the time to really enjoy the sunset, golfing, traveling or just doing whatever you felt like on the spur of the moment?

Whatever you have always wanted to do, now is the time to do it.

Ageless women are not ready to just stay home and bake cookies, pick up the knitting needles or start a third career as a permanent babysitter to the grandkids. Unless, of course, that is exactly what you want to do. Being an ageless woman is all about choice and free will. But I say, let someone else watch the grandkids for a few days and let's get out there and have some fun!

You don't need anyone's permission to live your life the way you see fit. You'll never be as young as you are right now. Get out that bucket list early and start crossing things off now. What are you waiting for? Let's get out there and give them something to talk about.

Remember, "Do not take life too seriously. You will never get out of it alive." (Elbert Hubbard).

Here are a few suggestions from my own personal bucket list. Many I've already crossed off and I'm happily working on the rest. Please feel free to add your personal bucket list items. Make your items as personal and specific as you can.

MARILYN'S BUCKET LIST:

- Go to Casablanca and say to Richard, "Here's looking at you, kid" and vice versa
- Swim with the dolphins in the Florida Keys
- Watch someone else (who I don't like very much) swim with the sharks
- Ride the mechanical bull at Gilley's in Texas
- Trek the Appalachian Trail
- See the Aurora Borealis
- Visit ALL the castles in Europe
- Shop on Rodeo Drive (with a really rich person's credit card)
- Tour all the wine vineyards in Napa Valley
- Dance at Carnivale in Rio De Janeiro
- Parachute out of a perfectly good plane without being pushed
- Learn Portuguese
- Go rock climbing (On a real mountain, not just in the gym)
- Take singing lessons
- Sing karaoke, but actually be good

- Visit Machu Picchu (Because it's so much fun to say it)
- Visit Djibouti (pronounced Ja'boo'te') (For the same reason)
- Be on a float in the Mardi Gras parade in New Orleans (and throw beads to the crowd)
- Perform stand-up comedy routine
- Sing in a nightclub act wearing a sequin dress
- Start my own charitable foundation
- Take a hot air balloon ride over the mountains
- Watch a lunar eclipse
- Watch the sunrise and sunset from an airplane on the same day
- Be a storm chaser for a day
- Climb an active volcano
- Stay at the "Ice" Hotel in Switzerland
- Stay at the same chalet that was in the movie *The Eiger Sanction*
- Learn to draw
- Learn to sew
- Write a book
- Be in a movie
- Be in a series of commercials
- Test drive a Ferrari (Red, of course)
- Buy a gold Mercedes or two or three
- Buy a red fox coat
- Feed the hungry at Thanksgiving
- Create and perform in my own music video
- Ride across the country on a Harley-Davidson
- Sit by a flowing stream and meditate
- Play in a waterfall
- Ride a carousel every day
- Bowl a 300 game
- Win a pool tournament
- Dance on a bar

- Travel to Rome, Paris and London
- Stay up all night watching Leones Meteor Shower with Richard
- Run the Jack Daniels marathon
- Put all my money on black at the Roulette wheel at the Golden Nugget in Vegas
- Put all my money on red at the Roulette wheel at the Golden Nugget in Vegas
- Watch the total eclipse of the sun (listening to the "Dark Side of the Moon")

This is just part of my bucket list. What's on yours?

THEY MIGHT BE TALKING ABOUT YOU IF:

- ❖ You're the first one to take the Polar Plunge (in your bikini).
- ❖ You have more dates on the weekend than your granddaughter.
- ❖ Your present boyfriend, Ricardo, is younger than your granddaughter.
- ❖ You posed for the "Over 50" pin-up cover girl calendar.
- ❖ You're blowing all your grandkids' inheritance on exotic travel, bad men and good wine.

Chapter 28
THE BEST IS YET TO COME
"Here Comes the Sun"

RICHARD AND I WENT TO a Three Dog Night concert this past year. When we went back to the hotel, the elevator attendant/valet asked how our night had been.

I told him how much fun we had at the Three Dog Night concert. He just looked at me as if I was speaking a dead language, which I guess I was. I was speaking English.

The kid had no clue what a three-dog night was.

Richard said, "It's probably what your babysitter used to listen to."

Then looking at him closer, I realized it's probably what his *mother's* babysitter used to listen to.

Don't you just hate it when life rudely, out of nowhere reminds you how old you really are?

But at any rate, back at the concert after they had played "Jeremiah was a Bullfrog" and "Never Been to Spain," they played one of their new songs. One of the original singers, who are all now in their sixties or seventies, introduced the song by saying it's about how as we get older, we quit looking forward in our life. We tend to think that all the best stuff has already happened.

The marriages, the births, the graduations, the promotions, and all the "highlights" of our life have come and gone. But their new song tells us that life still has some pleasant surprises in store for us. Don't dwell in the past, wishing you were still there or regretting what you did there. And don't waste the present by focusing on and complaining about your aches and pains, your finances or your spouse.

Remember how we discussed that what you think about is what you create? Have you ever noticed how people sit around and try to one up each other with their problems?

- "It's getting colder. I know my arthritis is going to flare up any day now."

- "My allergies are killing me with the change of seasons."
- "I'm going to be short again this month."
- "Why does the first of the month always get here before my check shows up?"
- "My sore knee always swells up when it rains."
- "I threw my back out again last night. I'm going to have to go to the chiropractor."
- "I have a brain tumor. I'm having surgery tomorrow." (Well, maybe we'll give this one a pass).

Why do we want to sit around dwelling on all these negative things? We are literally just asking for them to appear in our lives. (Just as we discovered in the chapter about "The Magic of the Law of Attraction.")

Instead, think of all the great things that are waiting for you in the future.

Change the above comments to:

- "I have an abundant life."
- "Physically I am in great shape."
- "My finances are in order and more money is coming to me now."
- "I am feeling good and getting better every day."

You are your own storyteller. Tell the story you want to live. You can enjoy perfect health, start a new career, find a new love, travel, feed the hungry, write a book, learn to sing, or perform a comedy routine. Or, like Three Dog Night, create a new album after 30 years.

A couple of months after the concert, I saw one of the lead singers on a CNBC business show. Honestly, I forgot exactly what he was doing on a television business show. Maybe he was there just promoting their new album. But what I loved was when one of the hosts jokingly asked him to sing a few bars of "Joy to the World," he didn't miss a beat. In fact, he belted out an entire verse.

I loved it! I don't think they actually expected him to do it.

He may be 65-plus years old, but he was totally in the moment enjoying his life and expecting a pleasant future.

We can be the same way. Our lives can continue to grow into something more in the future as we continue on our paths. We can develop our talents, find a way to give back and reach for our dreams.

I know I am an incurable optimist. But I also know that whatever my situation is, it's only temporary, even though people and circumstances may change. I know that things will always get better and that things will work out if that is what I believe. When I'm going through a difficult time, I repeat over and over, "This too shall pass" and it always done (eventually).

Life and the process of aging is not for sissies. As ageless women we have all lived through the good and the bad and the boring, the highs and the lows, and yes, even the pain and the ecstasy of life and death.

Each woman's experience will be unique to her own special quest. Each one of us has our very own lessons to learn. And each one of us has our own story to tell. But wherever that path leads us, we still have much more to offer the world and we still have some wonderful experiences ahead of us.

As we continue our journey of self-exploration, self-development, self-fulfillment, and ultimately, self-actualization, we know it will be an exciting one. As ageless women in the 21st century, we have so much to be grateful for in our past and our present and so much to expect from our future.

YOU MIGHT HAVE A BRIGHT FUTURE IF:

- ❖ You can't help but always see the good in others (even when it's invisible).
- ❖ You're an incurable optimist (especially when things are at their worst).
- ❖ You're always fully engaged in the present moment.
- ❖ You still have dreams that you look forward to fulfilling.
- ❖ You know that you are the storyteller of your own life.

Chapter 29
AIN'T NO STOPPING US NOW
The Retirement Revolution

OKAY, SO WE'RE ALL ADULTS now. In fact, most of us are over 50 or 60. We're the Baby Boomers.

We've had a good run. We've had our fun. It's time to gracefully hand over the reins to the next generations and fade into the sunset, right?

We'll get a nice beachfront condo right on the ocean. I mean, according to *Beachfront Bargain Hunt*, they're giving them away every day of the week.

We'll sip our cocktails and watch the sun set. Maybe play a little golf on Saturday. Perhaps a tennis match on Sunday. And tomorrow we'll get up and do it all again.

Sounds idyllic, doesn't it?

Wrong. It sounds boring with a capital B.

Do you think we really want to spend our days mindlessly wielding them away day after day until our brains turn to mesh? I mean, I like a good My-Tai or a Harvey Wallbanger and a beautiful sunset as much as the next guy. But I don't look forward to that being the highlight of my day each and every day and I'm betting you feel the same way.

As Baby Boomers, we are going to have a lot of years to fill after our "retirement" age has come and gone. I have a feeling we might get tired of a permanent vacation.

We want a life that is still full of exploration, excitement, stimulation, and anticipation of what is coming next.

There are still so many things for us to manifest for our future.

We as Baby Boomers have influenced society for an incredibly long period of time. Just because of our sheer numbers, we have been able to shape and create a world to our liking. Now that we're reaching our "golden years," I don't see any chance of this influence waning.

Just liked we showed the rest of the generations how to speed date, disco, raise a family, earn college degrees, advance in our careers, and achieve financial success, we are likely to show them how to spend their retirement years.

For many of us, the concept of retirement itself doesn't really seem that appealing. In the previous generations when someone retired at age 65, they had a life span of approximately 75 years. So it wasn't that daunting of a challenge to fill up just 10 more years.

Maybe retirement made more sense then. But today when we retire at age 65, we are likely to live another 20 years. That's a lot of golf or tennis games.

Many of us would prefer to stay more involved. Perhaps we choose to remain at our current jobs longer or maybe we retire from our current job but remain involved by doing contract work on an as needed basis. Or maybe we just go ahead and start a whole new career which has absolutely nothing in common with our previous job.

Maybe we just freelance, whether it's writing, engineering, or tutoring.

Perhaps we can use these years to fulfill our philanthropic side that we just didn't have time for when we were working for a living.

Or maybe we've not saved enough or blown all our money and we have to keep working at anything we can get. (The all too familiar dreaded Wal-Mart greeter dream).

Whichever our situation, it's likely that we will still be involved in contributing to society in some way instead of completely dropping out for good.

There's something about us Baby Boomers that we just have to do things our way. We've always been just a little bit out of the norm. We haven't just accepted things the way they are and moved on.

From the Civil Rights Movement in the '60s to Women's Liberation in the '70s and on to the age of Disco in the '80s, we have created and shaped our own destinies.

Whether we were burning our bras, earning our Ph.D.'s, driving around in our yuppie BMW, becoming the first female CEO of a major corporation or just disco dancing, we as ageless women have been an enormous influence on the past several decades and we will continue to impact the decades to come.

And we are seeing our future retirement years in a whole new light. Just as we drastically changed our status as women in the previous transitions, we will do the same in our retirement years. In fact, I believe that we will, and we are creating a new "retirement revolution" that isn't centered around golf, tennis, and sunbathing. We are molding our retirement in a way that only Baby Boomer ageless women can do.

Oh, I must go. *Beachfront Bargain Hunt* is coming on.

YOU MIGHT NOT BE READY FOR A 'TRADITIONAL" RETIREMENT IF:

- ❖ You have never swung a golf club.
- ❖ You're deathly afraid of the beach, ever since you saw the movie, *Jaws*.
- ❖ *Sharknado* hasn't helped.
- ❖ Ever since Serena Williams beat you so bad in that last tennis game, you have been too embarrassed to play.
- ❖ Then Vanessa made you look even worse.

Chapter 30
THE BATTLE OF THE SEXES
Guess Who Won?

SPEAKING OF PLAYING OR NOT playing tennis in retirement, I was watching a documentary last night featuring the legendary tennis player Billie Jean King.

I knew that she had practically single-handedly spearheaded women's tennis into the spotlight in the early '70s. I also knew she had won several Wimbledon championships. And I knew that she was a lesbian. But until I saw her life story and saw several clips of interviews from her career, I had no idea what a force of nature she was.

Her goal was to change the world and she did. She changed not only the world of sports, but she also changed the world for women in general.

She discovered tennis in her teens because her mother wouldn't let her play football with the boys any longer (because it wasn't ladylike). And once she held a tennis racket in her hand, she knew this was the sport for her. She told her mother almost immediately that she was going to be a world champion.

While still in high school, she won match after match and trophy after trophy. Then she continued her obsession with tennis into her college years.

While in college, she met and married another young college tennis player named Larry King (not THE Larry King). This Larry King just happened to be blond and totally gorgeous and apparently a nice guy, who was very supportive of her dream.

As Billie Jean's tennis career took on a life of its own, she became the face of women's tennis. She noticed how unfairly women in the game were being treated. In the same tennis tournament, the winner of the men's division would receive $12,000 while the women's champion would receive only $1,500.

The sponsors of the tournament refused to change the payout ratio, so Billie Jean and seven other female tennis players decided to withdraw and start their own championship tournament. They found a sponsor in Virginia Slims cigarettes and the tournament became the most successful women's tennis tour ever.

But it wasn't until 1972 that Billie Jean King became a household name thanks to the antics of an over-the-hill tennis player named Bobby Riggs.

Riggs, a self-proclaimed chauvinistic pig, had made the claim that he could beat any woman in tennis. Margaret Court, a champion player, had taken on his challenge (apparently for the money) and had lost to Riggs. So, Billie Jean, to defend the honor of women's tennis, had no choice but to accept Rigg's "invitation."

It was probably one of the most hyped and biggest productions in sporting events history. It was like the Super Bowl, the World Series and Barnum and Bailey Circus rolled into one. The event was called "The Battle of the Sexes."

(By the way, a movie by the same name, starring Emma Stone as Billie Jean King, was released in 2017.)

Billie Jean was carried out atop a throne full of feathers and jewels. Bobbie Riggs, who was always over the top, was surrounded by a bevy of beautiful women fans. But after the hype and the feathers had all died down, Billie Jean King had no problem proving once and for all who the better tennis player was. She won the "Battle of the Sexes." And she received a check for $100,000 (not bad for 1972) for her winning effort.

Billie Jean was now on top of the world. She had it all. She appeared as a guest on numerous talk shows, *The Sonny and Cher Show*, and even toured with Elton John, with whom she had become close friends.

She also had countless numbers of endorsements. She continued to push for equal rights for women in sports. But a few years later, her sexuality would put all this at risk.

A former assistant sued King for support during the time they'd had a sexual affair, which was early in King's career. Of course, during the trial all the details of their sexual liaison were made public, and it was destructive to her marriage and her career.

Even though the judge dismissed the case as blackmail, the damage was already done. The world was not ready for a gay tennis professional at the time.

She ended her long marriage with Larry King for the good of both of them. She wanted him to be free and felt it wasn't fair to either of them to stay in the relationship. But in so doing, King also advanced women's rights outside the sports arena.

She was probably one of the first, if not the first, female celebrity to "come out" as gay.

By the way, she has been in a meaningful and happy relationship now for years and today has the acceptance of her parents.

By following her dream in her career and in her life, Billie Jean King has certainly paved the way for so many women. She just would not accept things as they were and had the enthusiasm and the strength to do what needed to be done to change them. She said years earlier she was going to be champion and she was. She said she was going to change the world and she did.

Of course, Billie Jean King is just one of the many ageless women who paved the way for the rest of us today.

The movie *Hidden Figures* tells the up-until-then untold story of three African American women who played a vital role in the United States race into space.

In the early 1950s these three women were hired as mathematicians by NASA. They all were part of the mission team that helped launch the first U.S. astronaut into space.

But until the book and the movie came out telling their story, no one knew about their contributions. I know I certainly had never heard of them.

They were nicknamed "computers in skirts," but they were very well educated and accomplished women.

Katherine Johnson, who was somewhat of a child prodigy in math, graduated from college at the age of 18 and then went on to graduate school. John Glenn was so impressed with her that he trusted her calculations above that of the computer's and wanted her to verify the computer results before his launch into space.

Katherine Johnson continued to work for NASA for years as a mathematician and today is 100 years old. (Talk about an ageless woman).

Dorothy Vaughn paved the way for other minority women – and men – by becoming the first African American supervisor (of either sex) at NASA. She was a brilliant computer programmer and set up and ran the computer department for years at NASA.

Mary Jackson, who was also hired as a mathematician, later became the first African American engineer at NASA. In her later years, she worked in NASA's Equal Opportunity Office to help promote diversity hiring.

All these women were successful, but they had numerous hurdles to overcome to achieve that success. They had to use separate dining and bathroom areas at NASA because of segregation laws at the time. Katherine Johnson would have to travel to a separate building just to go the ladies' room because there was no ladies room for African American women in her building.

These women, who did the same work as male employees, were almost always paid less and rarely, if ever, considered for promotion.

When Mary Jackson wanted to take additional classes to help promote her career, she had to petition the Court to allow her to attend the local University, which was at the time an all-white school. She was able to get the Court's permission to attend classes, but only the night classes.

The successes of all these women seemed to be an uphill battle all the way. But their sheer determination to make it no matter the cost helped them accomplish what had never been done before.

Just as Billie Jean King changed the world around her, Katherine Johnson, Mary Jackson, and Dorothy Vaughn showed the rest of us how to reach for the stars figuratively and literally and for our dreams, even if they're "out of this world."

At the end of the Billie Jean King documentary, she was asked why she had done it all.

She replied, "I was tired of just getting the crumbs. I wanted my cake and the icing, too."

Isn't that what we all want?

YOU MIGHT WANT YOUR CAKE AND THE ICING, TOO IF:

❖ You think you can do anything as well or better than any man.

❖ You never know when to call it quits.

❖ You can envision things as you want them to be, not as they are.

❖ You're willing to bring others along on your journey.

- ❖ You know your dream is just as important as anyone else's (no matter how big or how small).
- ❖ You know that your dream can come true.
- ❖ You know your dream can change the world.

Chapter 31
HOW DO YOU LIKE ME NOW?
Now That I've Made it

WOW! WE'VE COME A LONG WAY on our journey in this book and in our lives as ageless women.

- We've discussed some of the best ways to keep our bodies and minds looking and feeling young, healthy, and vibrant.
- We've discovered how enough sleep, too much sun, a good diet and the right amount of exercise can affect how we look as we age.
- We're seen how even something as superficial as our wardrobe can knock years off our appearance.
- We have witnessed how believing in yourself and your dreams can keep you young.
- We've seen how important it is to have fun with life and enjoy each moment.
- We now know that what we don't do is what we regret more than what we do.
- We've even seen how under the right circumstances and environment, we can literally think ourselves young.
- We've looked at finances and investments.
- We've explored career options and advancement.
- We have looked at how important romance and companionship is to us as we age.

But we have gone even beyond the physical, mental, and emotional parts of our life.

We have endeavored to discover the true meaning of our lives on a spiritual level.

What becomes truly important to us as we age?

We have seen that what we truly believe about ourselves, and others is what is reflected in our lives.

If you want to know what you are thinking about, just look around. You are the one – the only one – who has created the world in which you find yourself. You create the world you see whether it's good or bad. It's your creation. You decide which one.

Your inner beauty begins to be reflected in your face and body. We develop that face that we have spent a lifetime creating. Superficial beauty is only skin deep, but true beauty is beneath the skin inside each of us. It is this beauty from within that sustains us in the long run and keeps us young. True beauty is at the deepest levels of our essence, and it endures. True beauty always survives.

Let that inner beauty shine through and it will keep you ageless.

EPILOGUE
BYE-BYE (For Now), MS. AGELESS
AMERICA

AGELESS WOMEN DO NOT MEASURE their lives in numbers. In fact, numbers mean very little to them. It may be the world's way of keeping track and measuring time and making judgments about us and our lives, but it is not something we notice or take seriously.

Instead, our lives are defined by how much happiness, accomplishments, laughter, love, gratitude, humor, satisfaction, appreciation, fulfillment, and self-actualization that we have flowing through our lives at any given time.

We are not concerned about the number of candles on our birthday cake, unless they are a fire hazard. The chronological progression of time is just a byproduct of time well spent. Ageless women live our lives so that we are much too busy fulfilling our dreams to hardly notice what year is arriving next. It is not time that makes us who we are. Instead, it is what we have done with that time.

Have we helped others along the way? Have we smiled and said hello to someone who really needed it that day? Have we extended our hand to someone in trouble? Have we shown strength of character? Have we lived a life on our own unique terms instead of following the crowd? Have we handled life's inevitable grief and pain with grace? And have we returned another's hate with love?

As I talked with women who were the inspiration for this book, I found that many of them looked much younger than their chronological years. But more importantly, I discovered it wasn't their appearances that most impressed me. Every single woman who had fooled the clock and had the "looks" of a much younger woman possessed a deeper inner quality that shone through from within. I believe this was what "caused" them to look so young, not the other way around.

There was a strength of character, an enthusiasm for life, a determination, and a refusal to give up on life no matter what the circumstances. Everyone had the ability to act upon life instead of letting life call the shots.

It's like they were saying, "You can't tell me how old I am and what I can do. You can't make me feel old, feeble, and frail. I am a strong, independent, and relevant woman. So, Life, just go on and mind your own business. I'm too busy to listen to your silly rules."

And by so doing they set Life and Time back on their respective derrieres by a decade or two.

Yesterday I went to take some of my antique dolls, some of which are more than a hundred years old, (talk about your ageless women) to have some repair and restoration work done on them.

The lady I was taking them to owned a doll shop for more than 30 years and had just recently retired. I knew that she is 90 years old and quite honestly was expecting someone who might have a little trouble getting around. Boy was I ever wrong! Ms. Paula was built and moved like a prima ballerina. Little did I know she was an ageless woman.

Yes, at 90 she does have some gray hair. Otherwise, I would not have had a clue about her age, either physically or mentally. She was certainly as physically active and mentally alert as I. She lives alone in a lovely third floor condo with a large terrace and stately old trees out in front.

The day I was there they were having problems with the elevator, so we walked up and down three flights of stairs – twice. By the second time, I was out of breath. She was not.

When she walked me out to my car at the end of the evening, she waltzed right past me like I was standing still. In my defense and in all fairness to me, she did have the advantage. She had a jewel-encrusted cane and I didn't. (Though I swear it was just a prop).

So, to Paula I say, "You go, girl."

To those of us who are already 90 or to all the rest of us who hope to one day make it that far and be in as good a shape as Ms. Paula, I say, "Make Life dance to YOUR tune, not the other way around."

I think we can trick Life and the ticking of the Aging clock, but not with creams, potions, and procedures that work on the outside. Instead, do just the opposite. Focus on the layers that lie underneath and that will in turn show on the outside.

I believe we have disproved that old wives' tale that beauty is only skin deep. Beauty goes all the way to the soul.

To all the Ms. Ageless American women who have been a part of this journey, it has been my pleasure and honor to be your guide. I would love to meet each one of you. Please feel free to share this information with the ageless women you know. And please be on the lookout for other Ms. Ageless American women. If you see a woman sitting at the end of the bar or sitting in a church pew or just sitting in the park and you think she looks forty-something, but there's something about her (like she has just a little too much class or there's a certain depth to her demeanor or she seems too wise for her years), she just might be a sixty-something Ms. Ageless American woman. Go up and introduce yourself and welcome her to the club - the Ms. Ageless America club.

THINGS THAT GET BETTER WITH AGE

- Ageless Women
- Classic Cars
- Fine Wine
- Art
- Rare Books
- Bars of Gold

- Antique Furniture
- Rare Coins
- Certificates of Deposit
- Old Money
- Antique Dolls
- Aged Bourbon
- 100-Year-Old Scotch
- Silver Coins
- Gold Coins
- Legacies
- Diamonds
- Philanthropy
- Stock Certificates
- True Beauty
- Antique Guns
- Antique Swords
- Grandfather Clocks
- Baseball Cards
- Real Estate
- Passion
- Purpose
- Relationships
- Love
- Health
- Spirituality
- Time Itself

AGELESS CELEBRITY WOMEN (We All Know)

- Susan Lucci
- Jane Seymour
- Tina Turner
- Dolly Parton
- Donna Mills

- Reba McEntire
- Faith Hill
- Shania Twain
- Joan Collins
- Frances Fisher
- Jacyln Smith
- Virginia Madsen
- Goldie Hawn
- Stevie Nicks
- Linda Ronstandt
- Nicole Kidman
- Julia Roberts
- Jennifer Lopez (49)
- Kelly Preston
- Annette Benning
- Rene Russo
- Cheryl Ladd
- Demi Moore
- Kim Basinger
- Christie Brinkley
- Julianne Moore
- Laura Linney
- Jean Smartt
- Dixie Carter
- Minnie Driver
- Michelle Pfeiffer
- Sharon Stone
- Suzanne Somers
- Sigourney Weaver
- Maria Shaver
- Melanie Griffith
- Teppi Hedron
- Annette O'Toole
- Candice Bergen
- Faith Ford

- Susan Sarandon
- Susan Blakely
- Laura Hutton
- Carol Alt
- Helen Mirren
- Glenn Close
- Julie Christie
- Katherine Ross
- Suzanne Pleshette
- Mary Frann
- Lynda Day George
- Julie Haggerty
- Marg Helgenberger
- Marilu Henner
- Mia Farrow
- Julie Adams
- Angela Lansbury
- Jennifer Beals
- Donna Dixon
- Kate Capshaw
- Cindy Crawford
- Vanna White
- Dyan Cannon
- Julia Duffy
- Linda Evans
- Rae Don Chong
- Bo Derek
- Ann Margaret
- Anne Archer
- Kate Mulgrew
- Nicole Michaels
- Tricia Helfer
- Darryl Hannah
- Kathy Ireland
- Brooke Shields

- Lucy Liu
- Marcia Cross
- Teri Hatcher
- Kim Cattrell
- Barbara Eden
- Lee Meriwether
- Gloria Reubens
- Connie Seleca
- Shirley MacLaine
- Raquel Welch
- Jane Fonda
- Angie Dickinson
- Hallie Berry
- Stephanie Powers
- Jill St. John
- Lynda Carter
- Julie Newmar
- Blythe Danner
- Meryl Streep
- Mary Steenburgen
- Sela Ward
- Pam Grier
- Cher
- Iman
- RuPaul
- Barbie (just turned 60)
- Ellen DeGeneres
- Kaitlyn Jenner
- Rita Hayworth
- Elizabeth Taylor
- Margaret Mead
- Marilyn Monroe
- Oprah Winfrey
- Mother Teresa
- Dr. Ruth

- Dr. Joyce Brothers
- Morgan Fairchild
- Bernadette Peters
- Loni Anderson
- Jan Smithers
- Diane Sawyer
- Paula Zahn
- Catherine Crier
- Deborah Norville
- Jane Pauley
- Diane Lane
- Nancy Pelosi
- Marsha Blackburn
- Gabby Gifford
- Hillary Rodham Clinton
- Geraldine Ferraro
- Sandra Day O'Conner
- Barbara Bush
- Laura Bush
- Nancy Reagan
- Michelle Obama
- Melania Trump (49)
- Jacqueline Kennedy Onassis
- Elle McPherson
- Courtney Cox
- Jennifer Anniston
- Lisa Kudrow
- Meg Ryan
- Helen Hunt
- Holly Hunter
- Jessica Lange
- Geena Davis
- Andie McDowell
- Jodie Foster
- Vanessa Williams

- Sally Fields
- Sissy Spacek
- Diane Keaton
- Bette Midler
- Mariska Hargitay
- Farrah Fawcett Majors
- Wilma Rudolph
- Susan B. Anthony
- Rosa Parks
- Florence Nightingale
- Amelia Earhart
- The "Unsinkable" Molly Brown
- Gloria Steinem
- Helen Gurley Brown
- Betty White
- Elizabeth Barrett Browning
- Natalie Schafer "Lovey" - Mrs. Thurston Howell III
- Tina Louise - Ginger
- Dawn Wells - Mary Anne

AGELESS WOMEN I KNOW

- Opal
- Teresa
- Jane
- Barbara
- Trisha
- Ashli
- Evonne
- Stephanie
- Sue
- Chastity
- Ava
- Kitty

- Chuckie
- Donna
- Laura
- Joyce
- Diane
- Diana
- Rachel
- Wendy
- Mary Anne
- Melissa
- Carol Anne
- Yvonne
- Helen
- Edna
- Sara
- Betty
- Pearl
- Linda
- Erin
- Patsy
- Angie
- Kimberly
- Candy
- Cindy
- Claudia
- Choline
- Sharon
- Karen
- Coley
- Little 'un
- Lori
- Pam
- Liz
- Janell
- Judy

- Janice
- Dorinda
- Cindy
- Melissa
- Cynthia
- Tracey
- Terry
- Gloria
- Carol
- Monique
- Jacqueline
- Conni
- Giselle
- Sydney
- Paula
- Sarah
- Susan
- Elaine
- Lana
- Carlenni
- Shelley
- Christie
- Kelly
- Edna
- Patricia
- Kerry
- Elise
- Sandy
- Teresa
- Regina
- Deanne
- Dixie
- Denise
- Dodie
- Angie

- Kathy
- Jackie
- Audrey
- Ranelle
- Jeanette
- Nancy
- Mandy
- Ruth
- Gail
- Katherine
- Debra
- Deborah
- Roz
- Ashleigh
- Sally
- Inez
- Cynthia
- Pat
- Patti
- Heather
- Patricia
- Mary
- Michelle
- Elizabeth
- Rebecca
- Marilyn
- Tanya
- Amy
- Alley
- L.B.
- C.J.
- Lindsey
- Cara
- Roxanne
- Rosanna

- Evelyn
- Jo
- Glo
- Jen
- Kim
- Trip
- Elisa
- Hensley
- Grace
- Macy
- Anna
- Abby
- Ridley
- Leslie
- Stacey
- Felicia
- Tammy
- Athena
- Johnni
- Robbie
- Ronni

AGELESS WOMEN YOU KNOW

Fill in this section with some ageless women you know, either in your life or they could be famous people.

ABOUT THE AUTHOR

Marilyn Gail Gaw is an author, beauty expert, fashion consultant, "ageless" model, spokesperson, and actress, who brings an eclectic view and expertise to the subject of aging. She has a unique perspective, combining style, fashion, and beauty experience, with a background in psychology and training.

Marilyn has years of experience as a consultant in the fashion and beauty industries representing many of America's top brands and designers, such as Vanity Fair, 1928 Jewelry, Savane, Tommy Hilfiger, Kenneth Cole, and Calvin Klein.

She has also worked in the corporate world as a communications specialist and educational representative for AT&T, traveled extensively as a trainer with Piedmont Airlines and taught college courses in Human Development, Self-image, and Self-actualization.

In addition to her work experience, Marilyn holds a Master's degree in Organizational and Human Development Psychology from Peabody College of Vanderbilt University, and has continued her post graduate work in Educational Psychology at the University of Tennessee.

Her expertise, education and example help bring to life the subject of "ageless women" who appear younger than their years, confident, self-reliant, successful, and independent.

Marilyn has a unique way of showing others how to integrate a beautiful and "ageless" self-image from the inside out.

.

Be on the lookout for Marilyn's next books, *Ms. Ageless Hollywood*, and *Ms. Ageless Royalty*, as we look at beauty around the world and through the ages.

www.ingramcontent.com/pod-product-compliance
Lightning Source LLC
Chambersburg PA
CBHW060318310326
41914CB00102B/1994/J